Anxiety Relief Mastery

Beat social anxiety, overcome panic attacks and increase self esteem with CBT

Michael Hewitt

© Copyright 2019 by Michael Hewitt - All rights reserved.

ISBN 978-0-6486577-3-6

This eBook is provided with the sole purpose of providing relevant information on a specific topic for which every reasonable effort has been made to ensure that it is both accurate and reasonable. Nevertheless, by purchasing this eBook, you consent to the fact that the author, as well as the publisher, are in no way experts on the topics contained herein, regardless of any claims as such that may be made within. As such, any suggestions or recommendations that are made within are done so purely for entertainment value. It is recommended that you always consult a professional prior to undertaking any of the advice or techniques discussed within.

This is a legally binding declaration that is considered both valid and fair by both the Committee of Publishers Association and the American Bar Association and should be considered as legally binding within the United States.

The reproduction, transmission, and duplication of any of the content found herein, including any specific or extended information will be done as an illegal act regardless of the end form the information ultimately takes. This includes copied versions of the work both physical, digital, and audio unless express consent of the Publisher is provided beforehand. Any additional rights reserved.

Furthermore, the information that can be found within the pages described forthwith shall be considered both accurate and truthful when it comes to the recounting of facts. As such, any use, correct or incorrect, of the provided information will render the Publisher free of responsibility as to the actions taken outside of their direct purview. Regardless, there are zero scenarios where the original author or the Publisher can be deemed liable in any fashion for any damages or hardships that may result from any of the information discussed herein.

Additionally, the information in the following pages is intended only for informational purposes and should thus be thought of as universal. As befitting its nature, it is presented without assurance regarding its prolonged validity or interim quality. Trademarks that are mentioned are done without written consent and can in no way be considered an endorsement from the trademark holder.

Table Of Contents

Introduction 1
Chapter 1: Understand The Different Forms Of Anxiety .. 2
   Social Anxiety Disorder 3
      Effective Therapy For Social Anxiety Disorder 4
   Generalized Anxiety Disorder 5
      Effective Treatments For GAD 6
   Panic Attacks Disorder 6
      Effective Treatments For Panic Attack Disorder 7
Chapter 2: Shyness Vs. Social Anxiety 9
Chapter 3: Symptoms Of Anxiety 13
   The Cost Of Anxiety 16
Chapter 4: Anxiety Is Not Your Problem 18
   Other Underlying Issues Of Anxiety 18
      Imbalances Or Gut Infections 18
      Thyroid Dysfunction 19
      Adrenal Fatigue 19
      Estrogen Dominance 19
      Autoimmune Disorders 20
      Cardiovascular Disease 20
Chapter 5: Back To The Past 21
   Habits That Contribute To Low Self-Esteem 21
   Bullying 23
   School Struggles 23
   Traumatic Events 23
   Religious Beliefs 24
   Social Media In Our Lives Today 24

Chapter 6: Fear Of Rejection 26
Coping Tools For Handling Rejection 28
Assess The Situation 28
Talk To Someone 29
Ask Yourself Questions 29
Walk Away From The Source Of Rejection 29

Chapter 7: Anticipation Is A Bitch 31
Coping Tactics 33

Chapter 8: Managing Stress 35
Work Stress 35
School Stress 36
Relationship And Family Stress 37
How The Mind And Body Connect With Stress 39
How Stress Can Affect You Long-Term 39
Forming New Habits 40

Chapter 9: Journaling 42
How To Get Started 42
Examples 43
Journaling For Anxiety 46

Chapter 10: Repetition 48
How To Begin 48

Chapter 11: Overcoming Location-Specific Social Anxiety 52
Party 52
The Office 54
Public Speaking 56
Shopping Centers 58

Chapter 12: Managing Small Talk 60
    What Is Small Talk? 60
    How To Make Small Talk 60
    How To End A Conversation 64
    How To Get Better At Small Talk 65

Chapter 13: Control Your Emotion State And Breathing . 67

Chapter 14: My Morning Routine 70
    Self-Care 70
    Breakfast 71
    Conversation 72
    Inspirational Music 72

Chapter 15: Don't Give A Shit 74
    Love Yourself 76
    Do Not Compare Yourself 76
    Strive For Intrinsic Motivation 76
    Take A Social Media Break 77

Chapter 16: Food And Anxiety 78
    Vitamin C 79
    Zinc 79
    Salmon 80
    Pink Himalayan Salt 80
    Avocado 81
    The Keto Diet 82
    Recipes 83
        Addicting Chicken - Keto Style 83
        Deviled Eggs With Bacon And Blue Cheese 85
        Keto Pizza 86

Chapter 17: Exercise And Anxiety 89
    Relationship Of Exercise To Anxiety Disorders 90
    Exercise As Part Of Therapy 90
        Walking 91
        Jogging 91
        Sports 91
        Gyms 92
        Online Workout Videos 92

Chapter 18: Moving Forward 93
Conclusion 98
References 99

Introduction

Congratulations on downloading *Anxiety Relief Mastery* and thank you for doing so.

The goal of this book is fast and sustainable stress reduction. It starts with a chapter that will help you get to know the types of anxiety and how they can affect you. This book will give you different options on how to get back to finding your center and finding peace, depending on where you are and how much time you have.

We will look into what anxiety is and what symptoms it often shows. We will discuss shyness, low self-esteem, difficult pasts, and how they relate to anxious feelings. I will provide concrete ways to decrease anxious feelings and live a significantly happier life. These tools include diet, exercise, breathing techniques, journaling, and even discovering the root cause of your struggle with mental illness.

With every tool i provide you with, i will show you how to use it in your own life. I will provide many examples from routines to sample dialogue. Overcoming mental illness can often be difficult, but I promise you that this book will make it as simple as possible.

There are a variety of books relating to this subject on the market, so i would like to thank you again for choosing this one. Every effort was made to ensure it is full of as much useful information as possible. Im not just the author of this book but I have also suffered from social anxiety in the past and these are the methods that I used to overcome it and although I still have little bouts of it from time to time the quality of my life and self confidence I now have is worlds apart from the man I was prior. I really hope that you enjoy this book and that your quality of life improves as mine did because of it.

Chapter 1
Understand the Different Forms of Anxiety

Most people that have experienced anxiety know that there is more than one type of this mental illness. These different types of anxiety can sometimes lead to depression and/or other conditions that affect the human brain. It is important for someone with anxiety to seek support whether it be from a friend, family member, or just someone you can confide in. If left untreated, your symptoms may not go away on their own and they can begin to take over your life.

This is something that I wish I acted on much sooner that I ever did. I kept it from my parents, my close friends and my wife. A big mistake as I believe bottling it up is what led to an eventual trigger of depression. If you take away one thing only from this book then please find someone to talk to.

If you have no one close to you who you feel that you can confide in, a professional mental health counselor is a good person to seek out. These counselors are thoroughly trained in how to help people who are in that exact same situation your in now. They know how to not only talk to you, but they know how to listen as well. They can point you toward the resources that will be the best benefit to your personal situation. Admitting this and seeking help if too often looked at as a sign of weakness or shame and this might be the first road block you have to overcome to get on top of this. Just remember you are not alone, you may think you are just your not, trust me.

Counselors can seem expensive, but even if you think you can't afford to see one, please still look into the possibility. There are many insurance programs that allow a certain number of free mental health counseling sessions each year. If insurance is not an option to allow you to see someone, look into free or reduced-price clinics in your area. There will always be a way to get help.

As for the help provided in this book, we will now look into the different types of anxiety disorders. They include social anxiety disorder, generalized anxiety disorder, and panic attack disorder. We will look into the characteristics of each of these types of mental illness. We will go over their symptoms and their possible causes and will discuss how to get help for each specific type of anxiety as well.

Social Anxiety Disorder

Generally, every person knows what it feels like to feel uncomfortable or nervous in a social situation. Maybe it is before a big presentation, maybe it has to do with public speaking or walking into a room full of people you don't know. Either way, most people can get through it. But it is actually much more common among people than we have been led to believe. Millions of people suffer from this traumatic condition every day, whether it's from this type of anxiety or one of the other forms.

Studies have revealed that social anxiety disorder is the third largest psychological disorder in the United States, right after depression and alcoholism. It is said that about 8% of the population suffers from social anxiety. It can be easily developed throughout life and later on as you develop more stress.

Situations in which people with social anxiety will experience emotional distress:

- Being watched while doing something
- Meeting people of authority (people considered "important")
- Most social encounters
- Being the center of attention
- Being introduced to new people
- Being teased or criticized by someone else
- Having to get up in front of a big group of people

General symptoms of anxiety:
- Racing heart
- Excessive sweating
- Turning red or blushing
- Intense fear
- Dry throat or mouth
- Muscle twitches (usually around the neck or face)
- Intense and constant anxiety is the most common symptom

Effective Therapy for Social Anxiety Disorder

One of the most effective treatments for social anxiety is cognitive behavioral therapy. Extensive research has proven that it can make positive permanent changes in the lives of people with anxiety. With that being said, social anxiety disorder can be overcome through persistence and consistency. Anyone can make progress against social anxiety when using the appropriate types of cognitive behavioral therapy.

If you want your therapy program for social anxiety to be successful, you need to address the dozens of strategies, methods, and concepts that will help people's brains to actually change. The brain is continuously absorbing information, irrational thoughts, and beliefs that can change as a result of a healthy cognitive process. An effective therapy program will supply you with the necessary and specific strategies you need to help you accept emotions, belief patterns, thoughts, and perceptions.

The first steps to overcoming anxiety:
- Becoming aware and understanding the problem
- Having the commitment to carry through with cognitive behavioral therapy even if it seems very hard to do
- Practice as much as you can so that methods become embedded in your brain on how to overcome your anxiety.

- o Try participating in a social anxiety therapy group, they can help you to gradually work on the problems at hand.

Generalized Anxiety Disorder

Anxiety is generally a normal part of life for most people. Worrying about the struggles of everyday life is experienced among almost every human being. People with GAD (generalized anxiety disorder) often feel overwhelmed with nervousness about everyday life and other things—even where there shouldn't be a reason to worry about them. If you have GAD, you may find it very difficult to control your anxiety and/or focus on every task. The good news about this disorder is that it can be treated in 1 or more ways.

Generalized Anxiety Disorder is often something that runs in the family, therefore, you can inherit the disorder. Doctors and researchers through studies have come to find that several areas of the brain play important roles in anxiety, such as the biological processes (the way your brain processes certain things). By learning how your brain and body function with anxiety, you may be able to find treatments that will work perfectly for you.

Generalized Anxiety Disorder is also extremely common. It is one of the mental illnesses that is dealt with the most often in our world today. Some people relate this common occurrence of the disorder to how busy our lives are today. They say that we are pushing ourselves too far and expecting too much from our lives, and that if we took time for self-care and we are realistic with our capabilities, we may struggle with this disorder less often. Others say that it may be related to diet and all of the processed and chemical filled foods that are in almost everyone's diets today. Either way, Generalized Anxiety Disorder is a real problem in our society and should be dealt with when its symptoms show.

Symptoms of generalized anxiety disorder:
- Stomach aches, headaches, muscle pains
- Getting irritated more easily
- Not being able to control your worrying
- A tremble or twitch
- Excessive sweating
- Worrying about unnecessary things such as catastrophes, war, or earthquakes
- Feelings of restlessness or trouble relaxing

Effective Treatments for GAD

Cognitive behavioral therapy can also be used to treat people with generalized anxiety disorder. This treatment can teach a person different ways of processing, behaving, and reacting to situations that may help the person feel less worried and less anxious

Medication is often recommended for this disorder as well. Your doctor may prescribe you something if they feel the need to. Doctors commonly use SSRIs and SNRIs to treat depression, but they can also be helpful for GAD, although they can take several weeks to actually start working. You may want to go over the side effects medications have before using them though. Some can have side effects that could make your problems worse. Discussing these things with your doctor is always the best way to go before diving into medication.

Panic Attacks Disorder

This disorder is often described as repeated panic attacks. A panic attack is often when someone constantly feels fear of disaster or is unable to control their panicky feelings, even when there is no real threat or danger. Physical reactions often come into play with panic attacks and can sometimes feel like a heart attack. They can occur at any time and people with the disorder often worry and dread the idea of having another panic attack.

Panic attack disorder can run in the family although no one knows for sure why some people in the family get it and why others don't. Just like other anxiety disorders, researchers and doctors have been led to believe that your biological processes play a key role in anxiety and fear. Learning about the way your brain works can be the best way to ease your mind and possibly clear up intense panic attacks.

Symptoms of panic attack disorder:

- Sudden feelings of having no control
- Fear of death during panic attacks
- Intense worry about when the next panic attack will occur
- Physical problems during attacks such as sweating, quivering, weakness, nausea, and a severely pounding or racing heart.
- Fear or avoidance of being in places where panic attacks have happened in the past.

Effective Treatments for Panic Attack Disorder

The treatments used for other anxiety disorders are the same treatments used for panic attack disorder. Cognitive behavioral therapy can go a long way, as can medication and/or talking to a therapist to learn ways of coping and managing your panic attacks. Always question your doctor to see what the best solution can be for you.

Another thing that can help with Panic Attack Anxiety Disorder is looking into your past to see where the panic attacks are stemming from. We will look into this technique in detail later in the book, but it is good for you to know that dealing with events of the past may significantly improve your life if you struggle with panic attacks.

However, if you have had a difficult life in your past and have panic attacks, it is important to look into whether or not they could be caused by something called PTSD or Post-Traumatic Stress Disorder.

Panic attacks caused by PTSD may be dealt with differently than those that are caused by Panic Attack Anxiety Disorder. To tell which one you may have, consider if the attacks bring you back to a traumatic experience that you have had in the past. Pay attention if you forget where you are during the attack or have no memory of the attack after it ends. These may be signs that your symptoms are related to PTSD. If you are unsure which disorder you are currently struggling with after reviewing the symptoms, a mental health professional would be a good person to turn to next.

No matter the type of anxiety that you are suffering, it is important that you pay attention to your symptoms and reach out for help. This is not a struggle that you need to go through alone. It's not, in fact, a struggle that you even need to continue to face. Throughout this book, we will give you tips and techniques that will help you to end your struggle with anxiety. Life is hard when you are dealing with anxiety and not treating its symptoms. It does not, however, need to be this hard for you.

Chapter 2
Shyness vs. Social Anxiety

There is a major difference between shyness and social anxiety. Shyness among some people does not affect their ability to make choices in life. Most people can even become comfortable with being shy. On the other hand, a person with social anxiety tends to beat themselves up because they have this condition and because it affects their everyday life so heavily.

Another difference between the two is that when you are just shy, the physical symptoms will eventually subside as you become more familiar and comfortable with the situation. As for social anxiety, the symptoms will not subside and they may even get worse. While shyness can sometimes turn into social anxiety, it isn't a natural progression. It is more of a mental progression.

Social anxiety is described as over analyzing things and hyper-focusing on certain things. People who have it may either re-live situations that have happened in the past over and over, often criticizing themselves. This often shows by the affected person playing conversations over in their head after they no longer should matter at all. They may look into what they said and wish or imagine that they had said something differently. They may even pick one specific word or stutter and be embarrassed by it. Often, the person that they were talking to would not have even noticed this mistake, but the person with social anxiety will not let themselves forget it for a long time.

People with social anxiety may also look back at conversations and feel sad that they were unable to express themselves in a way that they may have wanted to. For example, if they wanted to show that they had feelings for the person they were conversing with, but they could not bring themselves to do so. They may analyze every possible way in which they could have shared those feelings. This over-analyzing can often cause excess stress and even a lack of sleep in the affected person.

They may focus too much on the future and anticipate the feelings they will feel days, weeks, or years down the road. They may be anxious and worry about future events even though they know that their stresses will not make any difference in the outcome of the upcoming event.

They also are usually convinced that people will notice what they are going through and that the people may even judge them for it. Social anxiety disorder is most definitely a life-limiting condition. It can limit you from doing the things that you really want to do in your life. It can have physical symptoms in certain circumstances but it mainly creates real mental problems.

Social anxiety is most often undiagnosed; therefore, it can be left to grow and worsen for years. This happens under the misconception that there is no way out from it.

I do not want you to believe that there is no way out if you suffer from social anxiety. There are treatments for this type of anxiety. If you believe that your social struggles feel like they are more than shyness, please reach out and get the help that you need today. You will hear me say that time and time again throughout this book, I'm sorry if that becomes repetitive but to many people see asking for help as a sign of weakness and that has to stop. Again, life does not need to be as hard as it is right now for you.

There are no treatments for shyness, however. That is simply something you have to get over on your own. You may need some additional help to work on your shyness, but it is generally something you can overcome by yourself. If you believe your shyness is severe, you could try counseling or even just simple exercises that can help to overcome the feeling of being shy.

It is important to note that shyness is not the same thing as introversion. Being an introvert has had quite a media presence lately, to the point that almost everyone is trying to decide if they should label themselves as an introvert or an extrovert. Introversion means that you get your energy and your grounding sense from alone time while extroverts get this from interacting with others. It has nothing to do with being shy. Introverts can actually be very outgoing, but the talkative personality that they carry is not what energizes them.

Shyness, on the other hand, is feeling meek in front of others. It may cause you to not quite know what to say around other people, especially new people, or it might cause you to be quiet and not talk much to those around you. As you can see, this is very different from introversion. Shyness does not have to be a bad thing, either. Often times, being shy is a personality trait that is welcomed and loved by both the person who is shy and the people that love them.

Others may struggle with shyness. Luckily, shyness is something that is usually not very difficult to overcome. Shy people who want to be more outgoing can simply practice. When a shy person surrounds themselves with others and tries to be themselves instead of hiding, their shyness level can be lowered. If they continue to practice, they could eventually not feel shy in social situations anymore.

If shyness is something that you struggle with in ways that affect many parts of your daily life, however, it may be something more. Social Anxiety Disorder is often thought to be shyness by both the people that struggle with this mental illness as well as the people around them. Because of this, it is important to note that shyness is something that can be overcome with practice and it is something that typically does not interfere with how you live your life on a daily basis. If your shyness seems to be more than just a personality trait, consider speaking to a mental health professional about what you are dealing with.

Social Anxiety Disorder causes extreme amounts of fear. The people who struggle with this disorder often feel very uncomfortable or self-conscious in public places. They may be too worried to talk to a cashier in a store or even too afraid to eat when other people are looking. Social Anxiety Disorder can even cause physical symptoms such as the ones we looked at earlier in the book. It can be a debilitating mental illness to struggle with and shouldn't be taken lightly.

Though shyness and social anxiety can be similar, you should be able to tell the difference in what you are feeling if you carefully examine your symptoms. If it is just shyness, you should be able to help your struggles at home through simple techniques and strategies.

If your struggles seem more like social anxiety, first know that you are not alone. Also, know that even though your social anxieties tell you differently, you are not being judged when you are out in the public. No one is analyzing you from the way you walk or the way you speak. If you stutter in saying a word you wish you hadn't said, no one else is going to go home and think about the mistake. Social anxiety makes you believe that these things need to be analyzed but they do not. You deserve to feel happy and relaxed. You deserve to not worry about what other people think of you. Don't place so much value on what people you don't know think about you, life is too short to worry about that and this attitude will help you overcome some of the triggers that cause your anxiety in social settings. I will help you with the tips and techniques over the course of this book.

Chapter 3
Symptoms of Anxiety

Anyone that has experienced anxiety in their lifetime can easily tell you that it leaves you with behavioral, physical, and cognitive symptoms—all of which can be very overwhelming. Anxiety disorders are generally described as very intense and very persistent, making the symptoms very bothersome to most people. If you have anxiety, you may experience any number of these symptoms. For example, you could have a feeling of restlessness and chest pain and think that you are sick, but in reality, your symptoms could be caused by worry. For a different example, you could have every symptom on the list and have a type of anxiety that is extremely simple to diagnose.

I remember many times where I had a social event I had to go to or a meeting at work and I would be awake tossing and turning for hours in bed the night before. I would worry about every little thing that could go wrong, worried about what people would be saying about me behind my back, wanting to get there as early as possible so I didn't have a bunch of people look at me as I walked in. It was debilitating, I was worrying about things that were so far fetched they were never going to happen but I still found myself putting so much energy into stressing about them.

If you are having physical anxiety symptoms, it is important to be seen by your doctor to ensure that your body is healthy and that the symptoms that you believe are caused by anxiety are not, in fact, caused by a physical illness. An example of why you would want to be seen by a doctor would be chest pain. Chest pain is a very serious condition and can be a symptom of dangerous physical ailments. It can also come simply from feeling anxious. If you have chest pain, you will want a doctor to rule out the serious conditions before you start to call it a symptom of anxiety.

Other symptoms of anxiety are much easier to diagnose on your own. For example, if you are nervous in social situations and this causes you to sweat excessively and feel nauseous every time, it is probably caused by the anxiety disorder and not an additional physical problem. It is important to be smart when diagnosing your own symptoms and if you have any doubts or questions, ask a medical professional as soon as possible.

Here is the list of possible anxiety-related physical symptoms:

- Sweaty palms
- A feeling of restlessness
- Hot chills or cold sweats
- Muscle tension such as feeling shaky or trembling
- Constant butterflies
- Nausea
- Dizziness
- Racing heart
- Fatigue
- Shortness of breath
- Discomfort of chest pain

It is interesting that something that is happening inside of our minds can cause physical symptoms throughout the rest of our body. This actually happens from something called the flight or fight response. This is an automatic response that our body has and always has had. It tells the body what to do in situations that may seem dangerous to the mind. The anxiety symptoms are almost like warning signals being sent from the mind into the body to let it know that something is wrong. However, we know that we are not actually in danger like our mind may believe. Because of that, our anxiety symptoms can be caused by things that actually should not need to upset us in any way.

These symptoms can be experienced by a wide range of people. If you do not have an anxiety disorder at all and simply feel stressed one day more than you typically do, you may feel sweaty or have a fast heart beat. On the other hand, a person who actually experiences panic attacks will feel these symptoms as well. They will be well-known for the latter person, but they really can be felt by anyone. The physical symptoms of anxiety are definitely signs of the disorder, but they are not definite answers to the state of your mental health.

Another type of symptom that anxiety can cause is called a cognitive symptom. These are changes to the way that you think or to the way that your brain is working. These types of symptoms often come in the form of feelings or questioning what is happening to you. They can cause you to question your own symptoms or to question how others are viewing you.

Again, these questions can be normal and can have causes that do not stem from an actual anxiety disorder. If they have a significant negative impact on your life, however, they may be caused by mental illness. If you are consistently struggling with questions such as these, you may want to speak to a mental health professional.

Cognitive symptoms

"I am going crazy."

"What do these physical symptoms mean?"

"I must have certainty."

"What if ___ happens?"

"People will laugh at me."

"People are staring at me."

"Are they talking about me?"

The last type of symptom that anxiety can cause is called behavioral symptoms. Unlike the physical symptoms that affect how your body feels and the cognitive symptoms that affect how your brain thinks, these actually affect how you behave as a person. When behavior is caused by anxiety, you may not act like the person you want to be and you may not like the choices that you make. Try not to worry, though, because these choices do not define you. They are simply the outcome of the disorder that you are currently struggling with.

Below, we will go over what behavioral symptoms caused by anxiety can look like. Again, these choices are often normal. If you feel as if you struggle with these symptoms consistently then that is when you know you need to seek help.

Behavioral symptoms

- Avoiding situations that may cause you anxiety such as avoiding social situations like taking the stairs instead of the elevator
- Becoming heavily or overly attached to someone you feel safe with or an object you feel safe with
- Escaping from situations that you feel are giving you anxiety
- Engaging in risky and unhealthy behaviors
- Feeling pressured to limit your daily activities just so you don't have to interact

The Cost of Anxiety

These physical, behavioral, cognitive, and emotional symptoms of anxiety can certainly take their toll. Anxiety has a cost, and that cost can actually be very high. It can take away your comfortable lifestyle and leave you struggling daily with a wide variety of symptoms. It can cause you to be too anxious to excel in public situations. It can keep you home instead of being out and getting into the job or school that you dream about. It can cause difficulties in the relationships that you have with your family, friends, and significant other. It can even cause other physical ailments like heart disease, digestive issues, headaches, addiction, and even depression and in the absolute worst case scenario it can lead to suicide.

It is clear that the symptoms of anxiety can affect our lives in many ways. If you are struggling with any of these symptoms whether they are physical, cognitive, or behavioral, remember that life does not need to be this hard, everybody has difficulties and it's how you deal with them and the steps you out in place that can improve your situation. Throughout this book, I will offer many suggestions or ways to help you with this difficult diagnosis. You do not deserve to suffer from this disorder and doctors and counselors can help ease the difficulty in even the most severe of cases. Remember it's never too late.

Chapter 4
Anxiety is Not Your Problem

Most of the time, anxiety can be a disorder that was passed on to you by other family members. Often it is also an actual disorder that you have developed because of the way your brain processes things and the way your brain has processed things in the past. Sometimes, though, anxiety can be entirely just a defense mechanism against yourself, because you have low self-esteem, this was the case in my situation and it's something I have to actively work on even to this day at 37 years of age. For me it stems from my school life and bullying, this lead to the low self esteem which lead to the anxiety being around people. I worked hard at it though and as a result it's a lot better now so much so that it doesn't ruin my life anymore although I still have to be aware of it going forward..

A secure and confident relationship with yourself makes it less likely that you will suffer from developed anxiety and the conditions that come with it. Having low self-esteem can also cause you to suffer from many other disorders, another one being depression. If you are depressed because you do not have a firm connection with yourself, then you are more likely to have anxiety as well unfortunately anxiety and depression are like a one two punch, they go hand in hand. It is best to go see a doctor or therapist if this is the way you feel or if you know you need help.

Other Underlying Issues of Anxiety

Imbalances or gut infections

Lining the walls of your gut is a mesh-like network of neurons that causes sensations such as "nervous butterflies" and "a pit in your stomach"–feelings that are an innate part of your psychological stress response. As many as 90% of these cells carry information to your brain rather than receiving messages from it, making your gut as influential—or even more influential—to your mood as your head is. Chances are, if you're suffering from anxiety or other emotional distress, the answer lies in your gut. Here are some of the most common gut issues that may be behind your anxiety.

Thyroid dysfunction

Depression has been found to be an early warning sign of thyroid disease, including Hashimoto's and other forms of hypothyroidism. Meanwhile, hyperthyroidism (such as Graves' disease) could be behind your anxiety. Thyroid hormone is responsible for creating and regulating a number of important neurotransmitters related to your mood, including GABA, serotonin, and norepinephrine. These neurotransmitters can get out of whack if your thyroid is not functioning properly, triggering anxiety and panic attacks. Low levels of these neurotransmitters are also linked to depression, fibromyalgia, negative thoughts, and low self-esteem.

Adrenal fatigue

Your adrenals are primarily responsible for managing your stress response. However, when you are under chronic stress (as many of us are in this nonstop modern lifestyle), you can develop adrenal fatigue, where your adrenals are no longer able to keep up with your stress levels and they produce insufficient amounts of stress hormones. Caffeine can also be a major drain on the adrenals and can cause or worsen anxiety symptoms.

Estrogen dominance

Too much estrogen in your system is known as estrogen dominance. When you don't have enough progesterone to balance out your estrogen—think PMS and perimenopause—you go into raging witch mode where you can't control your emotions, which fluctuate wildly from one end of the spectrum to the other. Synthetic estrogens in particular (such as birth control and hormone replacement therapy) can cause both panic attacks and depression.

Estrogen dominance is due in part to the number of xenoestrogens we encounter daily in our modern lifestyle, including plastics, toxic beauty products, and heavy metals. Work on reducing your exposure to these synthetic estrogens while supporting your body's natural ability to clear estrogens from your system to help restore optimal hormone balance.

Autoimmune disorders

Chronic inflammation in your body can lead to autoimmunity, which may first manifest as a psychiatric problem. That's because the inflammation responsible for autoimmune and other inflammatory disorders (including rheumatoid arthritis, multiple sclerosis, and asthma) can also damage your brain and nervous tissues, leading to unexplained mood imbalances. With neurodegenerative conditions in particular, such as Parkinson's or multiple sclerosis, anxiety and depression can emerge years before neurological signs become apparent

Cardiovascular disease

It's no coincidence then that panic attacks exhibit many of the same symptoms as heart attacks, including chest pain, shortness of breath, sweating, nausea, lightheadedness, and a racing or pounding heart. While it is one of those "chicken or egg" scenarios, if you're experiencing symptoms of anxiety, it is extremely important to closely monitor your blood pressure, cholesterol, and endothelial health to rule out any underlying cardiovascular issues, and make any necessary changes to your diet and lifestyle habits to help reduce inflammation and oxidative stress.

Chapter 5
Back to the Past

When our self-esteem is low, we are at greater risk for depression and anxiety. Self-esteem is how we think of ourselves and you should always think positively about yourself. This is very hard for some people to achieve though. Self-acceptance is the next step and the key to living a more healthy and beautiful life without anxiety or depression.

Habits That Contribute to Low Self-Esteem

- Not trying new things just to avoid failing at them
- Constantly finding fault within yourself
- Ignoring important things you may need or want
- Procrastinating important things
- Refusing to forgive yourself for past mistakes
- Repeatedly doubting your instincts and decisions
- Always negatively comparing yourself to others

Once upon a time I ticked every one of these boxes and for many years. I missed out on so many things and experiences in my life all through my teens and 20s right into my 30s. Finally enough was enough and I got help, although I will never get those years back I have put steps on place to ensure the remainder of my life doesn't mirror this and so can you.

Comparing yourself to others is one of the main reasons for low self-esteem, whether in your favor or not. It may be helpful to think about why you need to compare yourself to someone else. When we compare ourselves in negative aspects, it may make you feel inferior, cause you to lose confidence, or make you start to think less highly of yourself. A very discouraging habit in the least.

Low self-esteem can cause you to develop a great fear of failing, making mistakes, or of looking foolish to others. You should never be afraid of these things because they happen among the average human being all the time. Making mistakes is always the first step in being successful at something. Every successful person in life failed a number of times first but they didn't get down on themselves they got back up dusted themselves off and went at it again.

Parents can be a large cause of anxiety in people, both when they are children and when they have already entered into adulthood. Stress can come from parents specifically if they do not approve of the lifestyle that their child is living. They may think that their child is not performing to the best of their abilities in work or in school. They may talk down to their child because of this. With this talking down, it is very common for the child to stop feeling like they are good enough and even for them to stop feeling like they are accepted at all by their loved ones. If the child is not loved and accepted, they will feel down about themselves. Since they are who they are and they cannot change how their parents view them, this often leads to extreme anxiety.

This stress can also come from parents who are simply not involved enough in the lives of their children. If the parents do not pay any attention to their children or if they seem to not care about them, the child will not learn to have confidence or a positive level of self-esteem. This can again lead to symptoms of anxiety for the children.

If parents constantly fight, it can be another cause for anxiety in their young children. The child may grow up believing that the fighting is because of something they said or did. They may believe that the fighting is happening because they are not good enough or they are not worthy of love enough. They may even stress over how they can get their parents to stop fighting. This is something that no child should ever have to worry about. When children do have to worry about this, though, anxiety often arises from the difficult situation that they are stuck in.

Bullying

If a child has a difficult home life in any way or in the ways we mentioned above for example, bullying can simply be too much to handle. If the child already struggles at home, struggling at school as well can be extremely difficult. It also means that the child has no support to help them with the bullying. Typically, parents could help with this. If they do not, the child has to deal with it on their own and dealing with such a large issue by themselves can cause many anxiety related issues to arise in their life. As I mentioned earlier in this book bullying was a problem for me at school. The worst part was my brother also bullied me at home about something that was pretty personal to me. Although my parents did pull him up about it they couldn't seem to completely stop it. As a result I never actually got a break from the bullying which only increased my anxiety.

School Struggles

School can be a challenging thing for many young people. It is full of tests and large workloads and it seems like the teachers always need you to do more than you actually have time for in the day. It also includes a lot of comparisons among students. If a child feels like they are not as good as their peers at a sport, subject or even body image then anxious feelings can start to build up. They can also worsen if there is simply too much work for the child to handle. Parents often set high goals for their children as well, when really what they need are the mental and emotional support to get them through their days at school.

Traumatic Events

Trauma can be a huge source of stress and often leads to a large case of anxiety. No matter what the traumatic event is, it can cause the person that went through it to feel like they have no control in their own life. When they feel this lack of control, anxiety and its many symptoms begin to take over. Trauma typically needs help from a mental health counselor to overcome. It is one of the most serious matters that can lead to anxiety.

Religious Beliefs

If you are in a position where you are practicing a religion that you do not fully believe in or understand, anxious feelings can be common as well. For example, if your parents are Catholic and they make you go to church with them, you may not agree with everything that the priest says. If you live your life doing something that he thinks is sinful, you may feel regret and stress over your actions. It is important to figure out if you truly believe in the religion that you are participating in. If you do not, consider looking into other belief systems. You do not want someone else's views to affect the anxiety symptoms that you feel in your own life.

Social Media in our Lives Today

Social media is a fairly new thing in our lives. Most of our parents did not grow up having this added stress in their life. This added stress comes because, on social media, people tend to post only the best parts of their lives. For example, they may post a picture of their beautiful family beginning to eat dinner in their perfectly clean and decorated dining room. They will not, however, post the mess on the floor after their toddler tries to feed themselves spaghetti. They will not post the dishes in the kitchen sink that have not been washed for three days or the dog that's barking at every sound while the family tries to enjoy their time together.

Because the poster does not show these behind-the-scenes images, you often believe that they have a perfect life. They obviously do not, however, but social media makes us see things differently.

When you see this perfect picture, you begin to compare it to your own life. The difference is that you can see the negative parts of your life. This might make you feel like you are not good enough or that others are living better and happier lives than you are. This can bring up a lot of issues that relate to anxiety.

Social media can even cause anxiety when you are trying to portray yourself as having the perfect life. You may go through experiences trying to take the perfect photo for Facebook or Instagram when really you should be enjoying the time with your family. You may worry about making sure others only see the good moments of your life so that you fit in with the current social media trends.

With these two stressors combined, social media is a cause for concern in the lives of many people. It may be new, but it really does give its users elevated levels of anxiety on a daily basis.

Chapter 6
Fear of Rejection

The fear of rejection, also known as fear of abandonment, is a very powerful fear. It can take a huge toll on how you feel and behave and make a significant impact on your life. It is common for people to feel some nerves when being placed in situations that may lead to rejection, but for some people, the fear can become crippling and really mess with their mental state. The fear of rejection tends to affect our ability to succeed in professional and personal situations such as marriage, job interviews, dating, business deals, and meeting new people.

When people are rejected, they feel something that we can almost describe as real pain. They feel embarrassed, anxious, and like they are simply not good enough. This pain is oftentimes enough to keep people from participating in the activities that they love. It can even keep people from accomplishing their goals.

This being said, people who experience social anxiety may feel the nerves that come with the possibility of rejection more than anyone else. It may cause them to not try new things. It may keep them from making new friends. It may even hold them in a job they dread going to just because they are afraid another job would never want them.

This type of fear is not fun to live with. It takes away a person's possibility of trading their current life for the life they have always wanted. Luckily, though, the fear of rejection does not have to keep a hold on your life. Help is available if you feel like you are struggling with this type of worry.

It is possible to overcome the fear of rejection and develop a better relationship with yourself. This should boost your self-confidence and make your fear of being rejected fade away. Whether you are dealing with the fear of rejection in your friendships, your career, or your relationships, there are methods you can use to gradually move forward.

As you can see, self-esteem plays a significant role in the fear of rejection. We will look into self-esteem and its relation to anxiety later on in this book. For now, let's look into times in your life that can lead to rejection.

Situations you may feel rejection in:

Work

Rejection in the workplace can come in many forms. If you apply for a job and are not chosen for the position, you may feel rejection. You may also feel rejected if a coworker gets a promotion before you do. These feelings can come from bosses that share criticism or from coworkers that disagree with your ideas. They can come from not getting the raise you think you deserve or from worries that you have in your mind about your job

Romantic Relationships

In romantic relationships, you may feel rejected if you ask a person on a date and they say no. You may feel rejected if your partner decides they want to break up. You may even feel rejection if you have not met anyone new for a while, thinking it's because no one would want to go out on a date with you.

Friendships

Rejection in friendships can be felt if a friend cuts contact with you or begins spending time with other people when they used to hang out mostly with you. Rejection can happen if you try to make new friends and it doesn't work out. Fear of these feelings can cause you to never try to make new friends, bringing on a much lonelier lifestyle for yourself.

Coping Tools for Handling Rejection

Rejection can be a very difficult thing to handle. As we have looked at so far, it can affect the lives of the people who experience it in many ways. It is a challenging thing to experience, but luckily there are ways to help if you happen to go through this often in your own life.

The tips that we will discuss below are all the things that may help if you are experiencing rejection or the fear of rejection today. They have all been tried and tested and i believe that they may help you to decrease struggle with rejection that you might currently be experiencing.

Try what you want from this list and if it doesn't work, try something else. Whether you take one of our suggestions or create your own, there will be a successful way in which you can deal with the fear of rejection. The first step in finding that perfect way for yourself personally is to simply start trying things to see if they work for you.

Assess the situation

If the rejection that you are feeling is not real, it may simply be a symptom of your social anxiety. If you are feeling like you have been rejected, look back at the situation objectively, try look at it as if it's someone else that went through that specific example of rejection. This can take the emotion out of it somewhat. Were you actually rejected? It could be that you were, but it is actually likely that you were not. If a person seemed dissatisfied with you because of the way they looked at you, maybe they were not and you simply read their expression wrong. Look back at the situation after you have calmed down and entered into a new location. You may just see a different side of the situation than the one that you were experiencing at the moment. Try your best not to jump straight to the worst case scenario. Often times, things will go much better than they seem in your mind. Do not let your anxiety ruin your chance at success.

Talk to someone

Talking to someone can help you to figure out if the rejection was real or if it was a symptom of social anxiety. It can also help you to understand and cope with the situation, even if it was a real rejection that you experienced. If you would like to talk to someone, consider reaching out to a mental health counselor. If this is not an option or if it is something that you are not comfortable with, you could also consider talking to a family member or a close friend. Remember that you are not alone in this battle. Like we mentioned earlier, your anxiety may cause you to see the worst case scenario when it is often not actually the case. This person that you speak to can help you to see the reality of the interaction with no anxiety clouding their judgment.

Ask yourself questions

If you struggled with a real rejection, ask yourself if it really was something that you need to be upset about. Did it really matter? Was it really worth the stress? Was it something you were actually qualified for or can you practice and try again another time? Be honest with the situation and with yourself and do not let your emotions get in the way. You may have anxiety telling you lies, but deep down you really do know the truth. Dig deep to find that truth, then allow it to improve your situation and remember failure is an essential part of success. When you fail you learn, your look at what you did right and continue to do them and what you did wrong and remove those from your next attempt.

Walk away from the source of rejection

When you are in a difficult situation, sometimes the best thing that you can do for yourself is to simply step away. Often times a new environment will help our body and mind to move on and to calm down. It can also give you some alone time to reflect if that is something that you feel like you may need. Take some time to think through what happened when your mind is calm. It is more likely that you will be able to see the truth of the situation if your anxiety is not getting the best of you at the time.

Social anxiety and the fear of rejection can be extremely hard. The next time that you are in a situation where you are afraid of rejection, try thinking back to the tips that you have read in this chapter. With you being the smart human being that you are along with these coping mechanisms, I believe that you will be able to beat that fear of rejection. I hope that these tiles allow you to get the job you've always dreamed of, the romantic relationship you've been working toward, and the friendships that you need in your life. I believe in you, and if you believe in yourself as well, I know that you will succeed in this challenging task.

Chapter 7
Anticipation is a Bitch

Anticipation signifies the beginning of expected relief. As you anticipate and expect more, you often get let down. Life will disappoint us because that is the way things work. Not everything will go in our favor even if we hope it will. As human beings, we do this with a lot of things. The end result can become translated into a horrible form of disappointment that happens all within our very own heads. If you are not anticipating things at such a high level, you are more likely to be happy with whatever the outcome happens to be. Unconscious anticipation can often get us exactly the opposite of what we are trying to get, unconscious fears can mess with the brain causing us to maybe miss specific steps that matter in getting what we want.

When you are in a constant state of anticipation, unknowingly or knowingly, you are also in a constant state of anxiety. Anticipation can turn into anxiety about the situation. If this continues, it can leave you with anxiety when waiting for almost any outcome or having expectations period.

Anticipatory anxiety is described as the fear and anxiety you experience before an event. It comes into play especially when you spend days, weeks, and months dreading the results of something.

For example, think back to a time when you had to take a test. Maybe this text was a big deal at the time. You may have even had to pass it in order to get the grade you desired in your class. Did you stay up all night studying even though you knew that the lack of sleep would not help you? Do you think that anxiety was part of the reason that your body could not rest?

You were possibly so worried about the test that it caused you anxiety. You may have had physical, cognitive, or behavioral symptoms. You probably stressed about the test for weeks and imagined how horrible it would be if you did not do as well as you were hoping.

Now, look at your life after that test. Was it really such a big deal that you needed to worry for weeks and stay up anxiously all night before it took place? Even if you failed it completely, did it affect your life as badly as you thought it would?

For most people and most situations, the answer to these questions would be "no". You did not need to worry and stress and stay up all night. The anxious feelings did not help the results and realistically, even if the results were bad, your life turned out just fine, the sun still came up the next day.

What about the last time you got a flu shot? Did you worry that it would cause you pain? Did you stiffen your arm, look away, and maybe even hold your breath? Did you even almost consider skipping your appointment? Then, when the needle went in and you felt what was basically not even a noticeable pinch, you probably realized that your anxiousness was not necessary.

In situations like this, the anticipation is much worse than the outcome. We need to remind ourselves of this when we feel anxious because of an upcoming event. Our fears are not necessary and we do not need to suffer through them.

Situations in which you may have anticipatory anxiety:
- Going on a date with someone
- Joining a new team or sport
- Preparing for an important interview
- Starting a new job
- Attending a party
- Going on vacation
- Oral presentations (this was a massive one for me), tests, projects

In addition to having anticipatory anxiety for specific situations or events, if you have panic disorder, anticipatory anxiety is a symptom of panic attacks that are ongoing. Panic attacks often result from the body misinterpreting sensations that are associated with the fight or flight reaction our mind gives off in stressful or dangerous situations.

The only way that you can truly get over anticipatory anxiety is by leaping into the things that made you fearful in the first place, rather than avoiding them like you have been. For example, if you are anxious about speaking in front of large audiences, you can try practicing whatever you are going to say as many times as you can until you've done it so much that you are completely used to it. Practice your speech in your room, then in front of a mirror, then in front of a friend who you know would never judge you for making a mistake. Build yourself up to the big event so that when the real thing finally comes, you have no reason at all to be afraid. Challenging your fears head-on can help you become less anxious.

Coping Tactics

Interrupt your thoughts when they are racing through your mind—interrupt them with something positive. Try to keep the harsh thoughts from taking over. You could even create a positive motto for yourself that you use in these specific situations. That way, you would always be prepared with a way to battle these difficult emotions.

Ask yourself if it is actually real. Simply ask yourself "is this realistic?" Perhaps, for example, asking these questions to yourself when you feel yourself stressing about if a tsunami will hit the one time you visit Florida. Obviously, if you asked yourself about the probability of the risk in this circumstance, you would have no real reason to worry.

Focus yourself on being positive. Try to draw your attention away from what you're negatively focused on. Go do something that will take your mind off of what it was on. Go for a walk or visit a close friend. Draw a picture, write a poem, listen to some music, exercise or take a hot bath. Do whatever activity relaxes you and brings you back to reality. If you do this same activity every time you start to stress about things that will not happen, it will help to ground your reactions and emotions right away. It will remind your body of how it can calm itself.

Assess the situation that you are analyzing. Assess the way you feel, what is making you feel that way, and how you can fix it. This technique can be very useful for the future. The next time you are feeling anxious about something similar, you will be able to think back to this analysis to see if what you are worrying about is realistic and worth it, or if you should be working on changing the topic on mind and calming your body down.

If accessing the situation doesn't help, try not accessing the situation. This sounds like common sense, but it truly can help in certain circumstances. For some people, being present in the moment of a panic attack can make the situation worse. Sometimes letting go can make the person feel better. In this case, let your mind take you to a place where you are comfortable and relaxed. Picture a warm, sunny beach or a peaceful walk in nature. Allow the images to calm your body and take you far away from the stressful reality until you are ready to deal with it again.

Lastly, always remember to relax. Many people decide to overlook "self-care time". Relaxing and giving yourself some time to unwind can really help with conditions like anticipatory anxiety. Calmness can push out negative energy. Do the things that you consider self-care. Consider exercising or meditation. Take a hot bath or snuggle with your pets. Indulge in your favorite treat and a good book. Maybe even consider taking a long, restful nap. Do anything that allows your body to relax and prepare itself to respond in a better manner the next time.

These tips should help you to cope next time you find yourself feeling anxiety situations in a time filled with anticipation. Remember that the anticipation is almost always much worse than the outcome. Remember to stay calm and to take care of yourself. You are capable of living in the moment and not living in the future, and your quality of life will increase significantly if you work on doing just that.

Chapter 8
Managing Stress

Anxiety and depression can easily arise from being stressed. Stress also enhances these disorders if you already have them. This is why it is important to treat your stress and make sure to keep the stress levels down because the long-term effects can be pretty harmful.

In order to treat your stress, you must know where it stems from. Things that are stressful to one person may not be stressful for another. Learning to break the patterns in your life that are related to stress can help you change for the better. Certain feelings, thoughts, and behaviors may have been fueling a sense of anxiety or feelings of being overwhelmed that have stuck with you.

There are different sources of stress for everybody and we will dive in some of the most common ones.

Work Stress

Work is the most common form of stress. For hundreds of years, work and stress have been directly related to each other. In fact, many health books have been made on the matter. Everybody wants to succeed in having a job because how well we do our job determines how much money we end up making, how we view ourselves, and how others view us. If you are employed then work is also where you spend most of your time.

Work is also how we make money. That causes it to be the stem of financial stress as well. We all know that money can cause huge issues in our lives. Homes, food, and basic necessities are expensive. If we cannot afford these, we worry constantly also if we are living pay cheque to pay cheque knowing that we have nothing extra in the back for when unexpected expenses arise or even enough put away for retirement.

Even if we can afford the common necessities for living a typical lifestyle, we still want more money to be able to do fun things. We want to buy things that make us happy and we want to take our families on vacations that will provide quality bonding time. We may want to see a movie or eat out for dinner. If we cannot do these things that we want to do, extra stress can be added to our lives as well. Money is still to this day a major stress in my life so I can fully relate to people in a similar position.

Both of these financial stresses lead back to work. We worry about getting enough hours or that perfect raise so that our quality of life can improve. We worry about finding a high paying job so that we can have all of the things we need and do all of the things we want to do. This affects our work performance, as well as the rest of our lives in a significant way.

Common sources of work stress are:

- Work that you don't engage much in
- Work that isn't challenging
- Not having enough control in your workspace
- Excessive workloads
- Few growth opportunities or advancements
- Low paying jobs
- Lack of support from the people around you

School Stress

Before work stresses enter our lives, school stresses fill in for the gaps they leave. We worry about getting good grades and passing our classes. We worry about learning the information that we will need to know in the future to get the jobs we dream of having. We even stress about how we will finish all of our coursework with so many assignments and so little time. Getting into the college we want is one of the biggest stresses a young person can face as in that present moment it can feel like our whole life depends on it.

Relationship and Family Stress

Even after leaving work and school for the day, the stress can follow us home. We may worry about if our children are happy and have everything they need. We may stress over a relationship that seems to be failing. Stress can follow us into the parts of our lives that are supposed to be happy. It can be found just about everywhere.

After reading this list, it is pretty clear that the less control you have over work, school, or family, the more likely you are to feel stressed out. It is understandable for your first few jobs to be stressful and unenjoyable, but when finding a job to settle down with, you really want to make sure you enjoy it and that it makes you happy. You want to make sure it does not give you stress that spreads into other areas of your life.

You may feel stressed at times even if you love what you do. Every demand of the modern workday can make you feel stressed and leave you looking for some kind of balance because your life feels out of place. Finding a balance in-between life and work can be interpreted into something different for every single person.

Finding a job with flexibility is one of the many ways people take more control of their life. Not a lot of people have the type of job that allows you to work remotely and comfortably, but if you do, maybe it is best to talk to your boss and change things up so that you enjoy your workplace more.

School stress is a little different since you typically don't get to just change schools if the one you are at is stressing you out. Things that may help with stress from school are time management skills to ensure you can complete your heavy workload on time. Try having a diary and setting your week out in advance, write down what you will do each day, what time of the day you will set aside for it and how long you will do it for. Being fully prepared and organized will help you to learn easily and to have less educational-related stress.

It can also help if you have a good group of friends at school. Laughing through struggles and having another person to help you who is going through the same things can make all the difference.

If time management, studying, and friends are not helping, try speaking to your guidance counselor. Talking through your situation with them may help or they may be able to point you toward resources that will make things easier for you.

Making a family situation where you have low levels of stress is equally, if not more important, to lowering your stress levels at work and school. When you go home to your family, you should be able to relax and not stress about relationship issues. One step in this is making sure you are with a person who makes you happy. Healthy relationships often have lower stress levels when compared to unhealthy relationships.

If your home is stressful, you could even consider family counseling. Sometimes a person who has an outside view on things can help you to see your situation as a whole and help you to make changes for the better.

Here are some physical symptoms of stress:
- Hyperventilation
- Frequent colds and/or infections
- Hot flashes
- Irritable bowel syndrome
- Muscle tension
- Lack of sexual desire
- Back and joint pain
- Rapid heartbeat
- Heartburn
- Jaw pain
- Muscle pain or soreness

- Constipation
- Headaches
- Sweats
- Ulcer

How the Mind and Body Connect with Stress

When it comes to the way that we experience stress, it is important to remember that your mind and body are not separate. These two parts of your being connect in more ways than one. It is highly unlikely that you will experience the physical symptoms of stress, yet not have the mental, emotional, and psychological effects. The connection between the mind and body relating to stress goes both ways. Your emotional reaction to severe stress may even release a hormone in your body that surpasses your immune system initially, making you more susceptible to getting sick. Just because stress happens in your mind doesn't mean it will not affect your life in many other ways.

In some instances, you may even realize the physical symptoms that come along with stress before you realize that some part of your life is causing you to struggle. You may get sick often, be tired, and irritable and then realize it may be because your job has been taking a toll on you emotionally. I went through a period where I was constantly getting a cold and also had regular headaches. This was also around the time I was having difficulty at work and felt trapped in a job I really wasn't enjoying.

How Stress Can Affect You Long-Term

Psychological, emotional, behavioral, and physical responses to stress are the short-term effects of stress, but if one endures high levels of stress for a long period of time, these short-term effects can put you at risk for long-term health problems. These health problems could really damage you and affect multiple areas of your life.

One of these health problems are mental illnesses. If you are stressed out for a long period of time, you could begin to struggle with a mental health problem like anxiety, depression, or panic attacks.

Other health issues could include a variety of stomach issues such as ulcers as well as other issues like headaches, irritable bowel syndrome or constipation. They can include sleep deprivation and overall body aches and pains. They could also include weight gain or weight loss depending on how your issues affect your appetite.

Forming New Habits

Forming new habits is essential in reducing your stress levels. The brain over time develops shortcuts without even thinking and we call these habits. Habits form after two connected behaviors have been related for so long, the brain stops making a decision about doing the behavior right after another. For example, you may begin of linking a shower to your everyday schedule right after you get off of work. This becomes a habit after a while and you end up taking a shower every single day as soon as you come home from work.

One good habit that lessens stress levels is exercise. We will look into this habit later in our book, but basically, it releases endorphins which in return help you to feel happier and more relaxed. It's a great way to take your stress and anger out in a healthy way and you will benefit by gaining increased energy, sleep and strength Exercise habits could range from simply going for a walk in the evenings to implementing a gym workout routine into your day.

Another good habit that helps with stress is eating right. When your body gets the proper nutrients, it is able to respond to stimulants in a better way. We will look into this in detail later in the book as well.

Self-care is a great way to help you when you feel stressed as well. When you are rested and able to participate in activities that you enjoy, as well as do things that make you feel relaxed, you are better able to take care of yourself in difficult situations.

Even though stress is different than anxiety disorders, we know that it can still be extremely difficult to deal with. We know that it can even lead to anxiety or other health issues if not properly handled. If you are going through a stressful stage in life, try using the tips that we have gone over in this chapter. I urge you to especially look at the exercise and diet tip as this was a major player in managing my stress levels and I have no doubt they will make a difference in your overall quality of life.

Chapter 9
Journaling

Journaling is a highly-used tool for stress management for a long list of reasons. Studies have been conducted showing the effectiveness of journaling for happiness, stress management, and good health (Smith, 2018). Not only is it an enjoyable technique, it really is quite simple, time efficient and affordable.

Keeping a journal to write in can be really beneficial for some people. Journaling can be an excellent way to deal with overwhelming feelings and emotions such as anxiety, stress, depression and it can be used as a healthy outlet in which you can manage your health and express yourself through writing.

Whenever you have a problem and you are feeling especially stressed out about it, try keeping a journal close by and try to document the things that could be causing your stress and/or anxiety. Once you have identified the things that make you stressed and can see a pattern in how you feel leading up to the point where your stress overwhelms you then you can develop a plan to resolve the stress in your life. Becoming aware is the first step and writing things down will make you accountable and aware of things that might normally just happen on autopilot without you even realizing it

How to Get Started

You can start the process of journaling by giving yourself 5 to 20 minutes every day to write about what is bothering you or what is weighing on your mind.

Write about your concerns. Write until you feel better about what is concerning you. Whether you prefer to write on a pad, a computer, or a journal, the act of noting your feelings will still be extremely beneficial. I do recommend using a good old pen and paper or journal ahead of a computer though, I personally think you get more out of it and take a bit more in if you actually write. This is just a personal opinion though.

Get into the details of what is happening in your life right now. You may be able to describe events that have happened recently. You may want to think back to possible events that have bothered you.

Try jotting down your fears and concerns for the time being and write in chronological order. Write down your concerns one by one and try to work through them by explaining what you think will happen next. If you are stressed about something you will naturally be thinking about the negative outcomes so try writing down some positive things as well that can come as a result of whatever it is that's stressing you out. After that, write about how each one will affect you.

You can also record your inspirations and insights for the time being and explore the things you want and the things that you need through writing in a journal. Writing down your goals is a lot more powerful than just leaving them in your head. Read through your journal daily and put actions to make them real!

I like to write positive quotes that I have heard from mentors or idols that put me in a positive state of mind. I have these at the front of my diary for quick reference.

Examples

Journaling does not need to be difficult. Feel free to use the tips that I have given in this book if you would like to, but if this information seems to be overwhelming, just try to start where you can, there are no hard rules to it. You may want to start by grabbing a pen and paper and simply write anything that you did throughout the day. Let's look at an example of this type of journaling together.

"Hey Journal, Alex here. Today I woke up and wished my alarm was not going off. I am still really tired, but tomorrow is Saturday so I am looking forward to sleeping in. I went to work today and got a lot done. We had a meeting and found out about some changes that are happening in the company. Then I got off work, picked up some groceries, and came home. I have been watching TV to relax and think I will get some sleep soon."

This type of journal entry does not go far into the details of how Alex is feeling, but it is a really good start. Simply writing down what happened over the course of your day can allow you to grow closer and closer to having a journal that benefits your life in huge ways. Also if you notice in this example he followed the negative of not wanting to get out of bed with the positive of getting a sleep in the next day. It reinforced a positive outcome to look forward to.

This journal entry may not seem very helpful, but as a person gets more and more experienced with writing down their thoughts, feelings, and daily happenings, more emotion will show through in their text. Let us look at what this journal entry written by Alex could have looked like after he had some experience with journaling.

"Hey Journal, Alex here. Today has been a day where I feel really tired. I did not want to wake up to my alarm this morning. I slept eight hours the night before so I should have been feeling okay. I am wondering if the reason that I did not want to wake up was because work has been hard lately and I was really dreading going in. Once I got up and went in, it did not feel so bad though. I got to work and made some progress. It does not feel like a success anymore like it used to though. I used to feel proud of myself for getting a lot done. The office has had a lot of negative energy lately and it is getting hard to ignore it. After lunch, we had a meeting. The boss told us about a bunch of new changes and most people are feeling stressed about them. I am feeling stressed about them too. I guess change is hard for me ever since my parents got a divorce when I was young. I will have to work on my feelings about that. I think it might help me deal better with change in the current times. I am an adult now, so I do not want past events like that holding me back. Maybe I can put in a journal entry about the divorce later, or talk with my counselor to help me let go of the anger and fear I have been holding onto since I was just a little kid. I think that doing that would help me to feel less afraid of change and be more positive in my life, even when work sucks. It would help me feel less stressed and happier about waking up on weekday mornings."

Do you see how different the two journal entries are? One simply shows the events that happened throughout Alex's day with no emotion or thought behind how he was feeling. The other entry tells in detail about the emotions that Alex was struggling with that day. It is clear that the second journal entry actually helped him to process some big things that were going on in his life.

The second journal entry did not only talk about his feelings caused by work on that specific day, it actually brought to mind a struggle that Alex had been dealing with for most of his life. It related his daily emotions to a difficult event from his childhood.

Without journaling, Alex may have never realized that the divorce his parents had when he was young was causing him to struggle with change. He may not have noticed that change at work was the reason why he was feeling like he hated a job that used to bring him a sense of satisfaction and pride.

Because writing in his journal brought this struggle to mind, Alex was able to face his difficulties and improve his quality of life. He realized that he needed to try to keep journaling his feelings and possibly even speak to a mental health professional about what he was going through. His journal brought him to the first step in the process of making his life happy and fulfilling again.

So again, journaling may not be much at first. When you start to write things down, events of your day may be the only things that come to your mind. Do not feel discouraged if this is the case. Keep writing down the happenings of your everyday life until something bigger comes to mind.

As you write down the small emotions that you feel, your body and brain will come more in tune with what you are actually struggling with in life. Things that never made sense to you before, you may now start to understand. Things that you thought were meaningless may be affecting your daily life. Things you thought you had to deal with every day for the rest of your life may be improved.

Keep writing things down and eventually, these big things will come out on paper. You will see things that you never saw before and be able to make positive changes in your life because of it. Remember to be completely honest in these diary entries though, it is for your eyes only so there is no need to hide anything. It will be good to go back and read entries from months or even years ago in the future and see how far you have come.

Journaling for Anxiety

Now, you have all of the tips that you need to start journaling and you know how it will help in the life of the average human being. How will it help you, though, if you struggle with anxiety?

Journaling can help with anxiety in many ways. First, it can be a grounding technique. When you write down the things that you are worrying about, you may be able to read them back to yourself and realize that they are things that do not matter at all. You may be able to read them and see a simple solution that was hard to find when the stressors were only in your head.

Journaling can also help anxiety by writing down when you feel anxious and what your day was like that could have caused your feelings. When you write down the different times that you become anxious, you may eventually find a pattern. You may see that your worst days come when you do not get enough sleep. If this is the case, your journal can help you to see that you would feel better every day if you make it a goal to get a healthy amount of sleep each night.

Journaling could show you that your anxiety worsens when you eat a lot of junk food. This could show you that if you try to focus on maintaining a healthy diet, you would feel less stressed than you do now.

Writing things down may even show you that your anxieties are worse when you spend time with a specific person. They may show you that you have an unhealthy romantic relationship or friendship. If this is the case, ending the toxic relationship will greatly decrease your anxiety and improve your life.

So far, we have seen that journaling can improve your life in many ways. We have seen that it is proven to lead to more happiness and less stress overall. We have seen that it can teach us about what is bothering us and it can help to calm anxiety. It can help us to process things that are too big to process in our own minds alone. Overall, journaling is a strong tool that can help anxiety and stress in many ways. I hope that the tips i have shared with you will allow you to implement journaling into your daily life. I hope that this addition makes a change for the better. I hope it is as great for you as it is for myself and that your anxiety decreased dramatically because of this powerful tool.

Chapter 10
Repetition

One of the most important steps of overcoming and managing anxiety is facing your fears head-on. It is normal for humans to want to avoid the things they fear; however, avoidance prevents you from discovering that the things you fear most maybe aren't as scary as you may think.

The initial process of facing your fears head-on is called exposure. The process of exposure to the fears you want to overcome involved gradually easing into a feared situation and repeating until you feel less anxious and fearful of the situation. Exposure has never proven to be dangerous for anyone and will not make your fear worse. After a while, your anxiety should naturally begin to go away or become less intense.

When beginning exposure, you should start with the situations that you are less scared of and work your way up to the situations that you are most afraid of. Over time, your confidence should build up and you should begin to enjoy the things you once were so afraid of or at the very least become comfortable enough with them that you don't get anxious thinking about them. The process often happens on its own. Exposure is the most effective way for most people to overcome their fears. It does take a lot of patience, dedication and planning, though.

How to Begin

Make a list

This is a great first step. Make a list of the things that you fear (objects, places, and situations) and try to make the list as specific as you can. Try to cover everything you are afraid of. Do not worry if you forget things, you can always go back to your list and add them in when you remember.

It can be scary to think of all of your fears at one time. Try not to be afraid. Have a friend or family member with you when you do this if you need some support. Remember that it is all in the process of eliminating the fears and that this process will help to improve your quality of life. There is no rush to get through the list and overcome each fear, take it at your own pace.

Build a ladder of fear

Once the list has been made, arrange the list from the situations you find least scary to the scariest. Rating the situations from 0-10 may be the best approach. Once you have rated each situation, you can then use the fear ladder to make an official list.

If you have a lot of fears, you may need to build different ladders for each fear theme. For example, you could have a list of fears about work. You could have a list of fears about personal relationships. You could also have a list of fears about being in public places. Anything that you feel which causes you many different fears may benefit from having its own personal list. Remember, these lists are not to judge you. They are here as tools to help you overcome your fear.

If having many lists is the case, each ladder should have an entire range of situations pertaining to each theme. Each ladder should also include steps that you can do with different levels of anxiety. It is important to take it slow and start on small situations and steps.

For example, if you are afraid to go grocery shopping, you should start by writing down each part of the experience that scares you. If deciding between brands of food causes a small amount of anxiety, but talking with the cashier causes a significant amount, rank the fears based on these feelings. Put steps into your list to overcome each of these fears. Do not worry if the list seems overwhelming. You do not have to complete the entire thing in one trip to the grocery store. You can take as much time as you need to overcome your fears in a healthy way. You want this process to be as easy as possible, while still being able to eliminate your fears.

Exposure training

Start with the situation that causes you the least amount of anxiety. Engage in that activity as many times as it takes until you start to feel less anxious when doing it. For example, if you have a fear of heights, try going and standing on a balcony or somewhere high up until your anxiety lessens. If the situation is very short in duration, try looping it and do it multiple times until anxiety has lessened. Find a balcony that's not overly high and slowly work your way up to higher ones as they become easier for you to handle.

Practice

It is important to practice and repeat these situations daily if you feel that you are able to. The only way you can overcome these fears is with repetition. Some steps can be practiced every day (taking an elevator, touching doorknobs, saying "hello" to more people, driving over bridges), while other steps can be done every once in a while (plane trip, presentations for work/school, swimming in the ocean). Just remember that the more you practice, the faster the fear will disappear.

Though the more practice the faster the fear will go away, make sure that you are comfortable enough while doing these activities to not make your fear worse. If you need to take things slow, please do. Overcoming fears can be difficult and you do not want to push yourself past your limits. This may actually cause fears to worsen instead of allowing them to improve.

Try to maintain the goals that you have created for yourself. Even if you become comfortable doing something, it is important to continue to expose yourself to your fear from time to time just so that the fear doesn't come back. You feel as though your efforts were all for nothing if this happens, so keep it a goal in your life to keep these fears away for good.

Rewarded behavior

Facing your fears is not the easiest thing to do. It is actually extremely difficult for most people. Reward yourself when you do expose yourself to them! It may even be helpful to use specific incentives as a motivation for you to achieve your goal. If you love chocolate, for example, have some ready for after the event. Also, remember the power of positive self-talk. Talking to yourself with enthusiasm and encouragement can really get you a long way. Repeat to yourself, "I can do this" "this is the new me" "I deserve to be free of this fear" the more you think like this the more you believe this and the more you will become that exact person.

Chapter 11
Overcoming Location-Specific Social Anxiety

Many people feel anxiety in specific locations. These locations can include places like parties, workplaces, or crowded public areas like shopping malls. Location-specific anxiety could include places where acts such as public speaking are necessary as well. There are many fears that could come about in these places.

These locations bring about social anxiety. When we looked at social anxiety earlier in the book, we learned a little about what it is and how to help it. Now, we are going to learn how to help it in very specific but common circumstances. Let's look in detail into each of these troublesome locations and how I can help when anxiety begins within their premises.

Party

One of the places where people with social anxiety tend to feel a lot of their symptoms are parties. Parties are crowded with many people. They are grounds for social interaction that you may need to either initiate or participate in. People with social anxiety may worry that they will not be comfortable talking with the people around them or they may behave in a way that later embarrasses them. These fears take away the person's ability to have fun and enjoy themselves at what is supposed to be a joyful gathering of friends.

Coping with your anxiety in situations like this can start with deciding whether or not this party is reasonable for you to attend. If you already have something planned the same day as the party, it is okay for you politely decline the party invitation, especially if you believe it is more than you can handle. Another reason your anxiety might spark up before a party is if you decide to attend last minute.

Maybe don't attend parties last minute if you have bad anxiety because there isn't much you can do about it. Deciding to go to a party last minute may take away from the time that you need to prepare yourself. This preparation time may be necessary if your social anxiety at parties is severe. You may feel more comfortable at parties when you have been able to prepare yourself for the event during the days that lead up to it.

If you are going to the party later in the day, begin thinking about how you can spend your time relaxing before the party. Make sure you have at least a few hours of downtime so that you can be with yourself and relax. You may also want to plan out what you are going to wear to the party, especially if there is a dress code. These steps can allow you to feel prepared for the party. If you dress well and feel good about how you look then you will hold yourself higher and have a lot more confidence to tackle the occasion which will show to others. If you are prepared, you may feel less anxious.

It may also help to picture the party in your mind. Who will be there and what will everyone be doing? If it is a party where you will be mingling with friends, you could try preparing some conversations to have on the top of your mind. That way, you can avoid anxiety during these conversations and always have something ready to talk about. This was a big one for me, I always found myself extremely anxious when in a conversation with someone. I found it ok at the start but as the back and forth conversing went on and found it hard to keep the conversation flowing leading to awkward silences. I had to work on this a a lot of practicing, researching and just forcing myself to speak to people. The good news is that it's something you can fix. Ask open ended questions and answer questions based off their answers. It's a skill no doubt but as all skills they can be learned and improved upon.

The Office

Having anxiety in your workplace can really put a damper on things and make you dislike your job. Getting stressed at work can generally happen to anyone, causing them to get anxiety. Although stress that is irrational and overwhelming can impair your daily functions and may mean you have an anxiety disorder, it is still manageable for most people. Here are some ways you can manage your stress and anxiety in the workplace:

- Educate yourself - Learn your symptoms and recognize when you are about to have one. This may help you handle any symptoms you may have at work. For example, if you feel your heart race and start to worry when you are growing close to a deadline at work, try to relax. Think about the big picture. Realistically, you will get the project done and turned in on time. Even if the worst case scenario happens and you are unable to finish your work, the punishment will likely not be so bad. There may be an awkward conversation with your boss about why you did not finish your work on time but after that, your work life will be right back to normal.

- Practice time management - Prioritize your work and try making to-do lists. These can help you to be organized and they can also help you to stay on task. Give yourself a schedule with an appropriate amount of time to get each of your work projects done. Keeping a consistent schedule that allows you to complete each task and/or project can really be beneficial. If you do not allow yourself enough time in your schedule, you will always be anxious about meeting deadlines that are impossible to reach. If you give yourself too much time, you may procrastinate and then stress about not getting enough work done in each day.

- Do your work - Stay busy at work. Do your job and maybe ask your boss to assign you more things. Working can be good for your self-esteem and it will give you good skills for the future. It can allow you to feel a sense of purpose and belonging. Even though most people dread work, it can actually benefit your life in many positive ways.

- o Tell a trusted coworker - Having someone that knows about your condition and accepts it can be relaxing and comforting, which can reduce panic attacks and anticipatory anxiety. You will know that this person is there for you and will always support you, even on the hardest days. Having a person on our side is a fundamental need for humans and having the person in the workplace can significantly help with social anxiety.

- o Ask for help - When feeling overwhelmed with work, ask one of your coworkers for some help. Maybe try returning the favor later on. The people that you work with are on your team and helping each other will, in the long run, benefit the whole office community. It will benefit anxiety levels as well when you know you are not alone.

- o Sales - The selling process when being a salesman is actually anything but easy. When it comes to pitching a service or product and dealing with the customers, many entrepreneurs struggle with a lot of factors. Some of them are fear of failure, lack of confidence, and fear of closing the deal with a customer. Professional entrepreneurs say that fears can be overcome with proper training, practice, and attitude. Sales can be an extremely hard job, but there are some things that can help.

- o Try having a partner or friend who also works in sales. This person can be someone you can confide in about the struggles you face as a salesman with anxiety. They can help you when you are having a hard day.

Try the tips in this book as well. The tools I have provided may be able to help you in your sales career when you feel forced to be social even though it scares you. If it does not help you, you could try speaking with a counselor or mental health professional. These people are trained to help you and can lead you back to happiness in your career even though you have fears.

As backward as it sounds, having work to do can decrease anxiety. It can give you a set project of things to accomplish that you know full well you are capable of. It takes your mind off of the things that cause you stress and brings up your level of self-esteem, which in turn decreases anxiety.

Public Speaking

If your job includes public speaking, it may bring about more location-specific anxiety than most workplaces. The symptoms that you experience from anxiety when speaking in public are the same symptoms that occur to those that have social anxiety disorder, but they are only experienced when speaking in public. Having public speaking anxiety may cause you to worry weeks before you have your presentation or speech, and you may have embarrassing and uncomfortable symptoms during the speech such as:

- o Blushing
- o Racing heart
- o A quivering voice that is usually noticeable
- o Shortness of breath
- o Upset stomach
- o Shaking from nervousness
- o Dizziness

In addition to getting treatment which is what most people do that have public speaking anxiety, there are a number of other ways you can cope with speech anxiety that will help you become a better public speaker overall. Public speaking is just like any other activity and preparing in advance will make your performance better. When more prepared, your confidence will be boosted and it will be easier to focus on getting your message out to your audience. Here are some ways you can personally improve on public speaking:

- o Make sure to choose a topic that interests you - If you are able to choose your own topic, try choosing one that you are interested in and maybe already have knowledge on. If you are not able to choose your own topic, try picking the one that you find the most interesting. This will ensure that you are motivated and engaged in your topic enough to prepare with research and practice.your passion for the topic will show through keeping your audience engaged.

- Become familiar with where you are giving the speech - Try to visit the place you will be speaking at beforehand. If possible, try practicing your speech at least once in the environment that you will be speaking in, and therefore, you will become more comfortable with the area initially, making your speech a lot easier for you to perform in front of a crowd. This will give you a lot less to worry about once your time comes.

- Ask for criticism on your speech - Asking others for accommodations can help you to control your anxiety. If there is something that would make you more comfortable while doing your speech, see if the change can be made. Whatever may make it easier for you to manage your anxiety during the speech, see if it can be accommodated.

- Don't script your speech - Instead of reading your entire speech from a piece of paper, try preparing a list of key points that you can refer to. This will be the best option because if you have practiced and memorized your speech, then you shouldn't need to read it from a piece of paper word by word and this will boost your confidence as well. It will make the speech sound more natural, I know when I give one if I have the entire speech in front of me I have a tendency to read straight off the paper and as a result I race through it at 100 miles per hour and I come off as nervous which increases my anxiety.

Shopping Centers

While shopping is therapeutic to some, to others it may be extremely stressful. It can be an unpleasant experience for people with anxiety. The main reasons people get anxious in stores are huge crowds, loud music, and assistance from the worker. These things can leave shoppers feeling worked up. Here are some ways to handle stress that shopping may cause:

- Make a plan before going out to shop - This could range from planning where you are going to shop to making a list of the items you want to purchase while at the store. Knowing these variables can really help you in advance.

- Bring a friend along - Having someone with you while shopping can really help to keep you grounded. Friends can also encourage you and add onto feeling better about being in an unknown environment.

- Discover where your anxiety stems from - Anxiety isn't only a disorder you are born with or that is passed down to you from ancestors. Having anxiety can sometimes mean that you are not comfortable with something in your life, or maybe you are anxious about something in your life and you begin manifesting it. Developing breathing techniques to manage your anxiety is the first step in the right direction.

- Shop in an outlet you feel more comfortable - If you are planning to go to the biggest mall in the city, and that mall makes you super uncomfortable, maybe try shopping in a quieter and smaller environment. Although doing this can sometimes make you feel as though you are also in a controlled environment, which is not what you want when you have anxiety.

- Try not to be afraid to ask for help - Asking for help is sometimes very hard, especially for people with social anxiety. It can be stressful but do not let it control you. Remember that you are the customer and if you have a problem, it is their job to solve it, not yours.

- Facing fears - People with anxiety sometimes try to avoid the places where they have become anxious in the past. People with panic attacks can have serious symptoms. If this explains your location-specific anxiety, read our chapter about facing fears. It is full of tools that may help your specific situation.

Overall, it is clear that location-specific anxiety is common and that it is a difficult thing to deal with. However, if you have the right tools, we are sure that you will be able to overcome this social struggle.

Chapter 12
Managing Small Talk

Small talk is a huge part of the lives we live today. It is a necessary type of communication for situations that range from interacting with the grocery store cashier who is ringing up your purchase to getting to know the businessman who you aim to score a big deal with.

Without small talk, our lives can be challenging. However, small talk is actually something that many of us struggle with today. People who have an anxiety disorder, are shy, or are introverted may struggle with small talk even more.

Why is small talk so difficult for most people? Its difficulty probably stems from the fact that it is awkward. These little conversations typically are performed with people who we do not know well. They are usually on topics that have little to no meaning. They are also quite random, so it can be hard to think of what to say when small talk situations arise.

What is Small Talk?

Small talk is typically described as meaningless conversations meant to fill time with someone you do not know well. It could also be a means to start getting to know a new person. Either way, it can be difficult and awkward for all members of the conversation.

How to Make Small Talk

1. Ask questions - When you are getting into small talk, one of the hardest parts is figuring out what in the world you are going to talk about. One way to solve this problem is by asking questions. You could even have a list of questions ready in your mind for when the time to use them arises. When you ask

these questions, you will be encouraging the other person to talk. This takes a lot of the pressure in the conversation off of you.

2. Listen - When the person is talking, make sure you are listening well. Make eye contact with them and act interested in what they have to say, whether you are actually interested or not. This will make the person talking more comfortable and will probably help to keep them talking longer. This once again takes pressure away from you during the talk.

3. Be in the moment - Our culture tends to be extremely hooked onto our smartphones. We have them with us no matter where we are or what we are doing. We tend to scroll through social media on them or play games even when we should be conversing with the people around us. We may not even notice we are doing this at times because it is such a habit. When you are engaging in small talk, however, try your best to not look at your phone at all. This will not only keep you engaged in the conversation, but it will show the other person that you are committed to the talk as well. Also, if you are on your phone, you could stop listening to the person you are conversing with, which could lead to some awkward and stressful situations.

4. Get excited - Like we said earlier, whether you are interested in the conversation or not, make sure you act excited. If you are happy about the topic and engaged in the conversation, it will feel better for the person who you are talking to. This will help to allow the small talk to serve its purpose and help the other person feel more comfortable and excited to contribute to the conversation as well. Both of these things will help to lessen anxiety levels during the talk.

Even with these four tips, you may need some additional help in having a successful small talk conversation. Another thing that can help in significant ways is to have some conversation topics ready to discuss in case that dreaded awkward silence begins to arise. Below, we will look into what some of these prepared topics could be.

1) The location or the venue

If you are in a cool place, it is something that both you and the person who you are talking to are experiencing together. Talk about how great it is. Mention the fun things around you or the beautiful sights. This commonality is something that anyone would feel comfortable discussing, so it is an easy go-to subject. It is also an easy topic to remember since all you need to do is look around to come up with the subject matter.

2) Entertainment

Entertainment is something that many people have in common as well. Think of a commercial you have seen lately about an interesting film, and ask the person if they have seen the movie. Talk about a popular film or a play that is coming to town. Even if the person has different interests than you, they will likely have at least heard of what you are talking about through the media and be able to discuss it with you for some time.

3) Art

If the person you are talking to is into art, it can be a great topic to bring up. It is a subject that has extremely passionate followers so this topic can lead to long and meaningful conversations.

4) Food

This is a great subject to start a small talk conversation with because everyone loves food. It is proven to be a subject that brings people together. People are also very passionate about their foods. For example, if you and this person are both vegetarian, you would be able to discuss eating habits for hours. Also, if you know that someone eats in a special way like by following the ketogenic diet, they may be able to spend quite a while explaining this and its purpose to you.

You can also simply bond by talking about great food. Talk about a dessert that almost everyone likes, such as chocolate or ice cream. Most people like to talk about yummy foods.

5) Hobbies

If you have a similar hobby to the person who you are talking to, this can be a great topic. For example, if you both own horses, you could go on with the subject for hours. This topic also works if you know that they have any interesting hobbies that you do not know much about. They will likely love to explain their pastime to you. Make sure that it is something that is public knowledge, though, because you do not want to come off as being creepy for knowing too much about their personal life.

6) Work

You do not want this conversation to be boring, but if you have similar jobs, it can be a great connection piece to begin small talk with. Try to stay positive and talk about things that you likely both experience at work. There is a good chance that this will give the other person in the conversation a lot to talk about as well.

7) Sports

This topic can be a little tricky, but if you find the right person, they will love to talk to you about this for hours. You will want to use this topic when you know or at least feel pretty confident that the person you are talking to has an interest in sports. If they do not, the conversation will likely not be a great one.

You will also want to be careful that you do not bash the person's favorite team. If they are wearing a jersey from the losing Super Bowl team, maybe do not mention how great you thought the big game was. For initial small talk, try to either be on their side or to not take sides at all.

8) The weather

If you are living in a place with extreme weather or are on the brink of a season change, this is a great topic to start a small talk conversation with and also probably the most common. It is a topic that every single person around you has in common with you. Every person that lives close to you is experiencing the same weather as you, so it is something that is almost always easy to talk about. It is the go-to small talk conversation that most people start out with if they need a topic to break through that awkward silence.

The person that you are talking to may not agree with you or feel the same way about the weather as you feel, but that is fine. Weather is a topic that most people are passionate about. For example, people either hate the snow or love the snow. If you bring up a snowstorm to an acquaintance, they may talk about their love for it or how upset they are that it is happening. With this topic, you can either have an immediate connection about how you feel, or you can have a friendly debate.

How to End a Conversation

Of course, it is important to know what to say while participating in a small talk conversation like we have been talking about in this chapter so far, but it is also important to know how to end a conversation. Whether you are no longer comfortable in the conversation, are not sure what else to say, or if it is time for you to leave, you do not want to just walk away without saying anything. You also do not want to say goodbye out of nowhere because it may come across as very awkward. You will need some ways in your mind to exit the conversation.

First, try to tell the person how great it was talking to them. Tell them that you have had a great conversation and hope to talk to them again sometime soon. This will cue the person on the fact that you need to leave and they may even help to end the conversation.

If you need to go somewhere, you may even be able to simply but politely tell the person that it is time for you to leave. They will likely understand and accept this as a goodbye since the small talk was likely just filling a gap in time anyway.

You may need to be a little clearer if they do not get these hints. Say "It was nice talking to you, hope you have a great rest of your day!" or something similar to this. Then give them a polite smile and walk away.

Of course, always do these things when there is a natural break in the conversation. It will feel awkward or rude if you leave while the other person is talking or when a topic is not yet finished.

How to Get Better at Small Talk

Most people are bad at small talk when they first start to participate in it. This is especially true if you suffer from social anxiety, fear of rejection, a lack of confidence, or low self-esteem. However, if you follow these tips, you will be able to get better at it every time you try.

1. Look for opportunities to make small talk - The best way to get better at small talk is simply by doing it. If you do not participate in small talk and continue to think about it, you will continue to worry and stress about it. This will cause you to be anxious when trying to have a small talk conversation, and we know that being anxious in this situation is not helpful.

2. That being said, just go out and try to have small talk conversations with the people around you. Do not feel bad if the conversations do not go well. Simply move on and try again. Eventually, after enough practice, you will master this skill.

3. Pretend you're speaking to a friend - If you are still feeling nervous, pretend you know the person really well. If you can convince yourself that there is no reason to be shy or anxious, the conversation is sure to go smoothly.

4. Give yourself a break - Like we mentioned earlier, do not worry if the conversation goes bad. If you mix up some words or have a few moments of awkward silence, just move forward with the conversation. We are our own worst critics, so it is likely that the person who you are talking to will not even notice.

5. Set a goal - Decide what you would like to get out of this conversation. Maybe try starting with a small goal. If it is your goal to simply start a conversation, you will get a boost of confidence after succeeding. Making your goals slowly

become more challenging until your small talk leads to real things, even things as big as new relationships or friendships.

Try not to mention topics that can be controversial. For example, do not say anything that is inappropriate. It may offend the person that you are talking to since you do not know them well enough to understand what they are offended by. Try not to mention religion or politics, as you do not want to start a fight during your small talk. Talking about happier and less controversial issues will always go over smoothly when these topics likely will not.

It can even sometimes be a good idea to avoid small talk altogether. The times when you should avoid it are the times that you are not ready to converse in this manner or the times that you are feeling nervous. You want to feel happy, confident, and ready to go into these conversations. If small talk is what you actually want to be doing, it will be much more successful in the end.

Right now, it may seem like you will never want to participate in small talk or if you do want to, it might feel like you will never be ready. Simply try my tips if this is how you feel. I believe that they truly will be able to help you in your journey toward mastering the art of small talk as they have mine.

Making small talk can be an extremely difficult thing to do, however, it is possible. Even if you struggle with social anxiety or a fear of rejection, small talk is something that you will be able to handle if you practice and prepare yourself. Follow the tips that i have gone over in this chapter. Have some ideas of topics ready in your mind. Make sure that they are relatable and not controversial. If you follow these tips, you will be able to handle small talk better than ever before.

Chapter 13
Control Your Emotion State and Breathing

We all know that our emotions can get the best of us at times. Our stress or anxiety can almost take over our lives. If you are feeling overwhelmed and having many physical symptoms of anxiety, you will definitely be looking for anything that you can do to help your mind and body to relax. One of the best things that you can do to add relaxation to your day is to look at your breathing.

Breathing is such a simple thing. We know that we need to do this act every minute of every day in order to keep our bodies alive. Breathing is basically second nature and we often do not think about it while we are doing it. Why is it then that when we are stressed or anxious, we often forget to breathe?

When you begin to focus on your breathing, it reminds you that you are fully in charge of your body. Your breathing can help you to calm down and it can even help you to lessen symptoms of great stress and anxiety. We will now look into a few different breathing techniques that can help you to calm yourself in times of distress.

Swami Swatmarama wrote on the practice of Pranayama in the original text of Hatha Yoga Pradipika, "When breath is unsteady, the mind is unsteady. When the breath is steady, the mind is steady". Therefore, one should restrain the breath (Swatmarama, 1500)".

This breathing pattern is meant to calm your mind and body down. It is comfortable to perform this exercise while either laying down or sitting on the ground. You will want to be in a position that allows you to be comfortable but also allows you to sit with good form and posture. You will also want your body to be in a position that allows you to focus on your breathing, as that is the main point in this exercise.

1. Place a fingertip lightly on your right nostril and inhale through the left.
2. Hold for as long as possible.
3. Release fingertip and place on left nostril while you exhale through the right nostril.
4. Inhale slowly through the right nostril.
5. Hold for as long as possible.
6. Release fingertip and place on right nostril while you exhale through the left.

When you are doing this breathing pattern, consider repeating it either four or five times. The more times that you do it, the more your mind and body will relax.

If you are not into Yoga or ancient remedies, there are many breathing techniques that are commonly used to ease anxiety in today's time as well. One of these techniques is as follows:

- Breathe in through your nose
- Breathe out through your mouth

How simple, right? Breathing in this way can help you to calm your emotions while grounding yourself and bringing you away from anxiety and back to reality.

Here is another calming breathing technique:

- Breathe in for five seconds
- Hold your breath for three seconds
- Breathe out for five seconds

This tip is so relaxing that many people even use it to fall asleep quickly. It releases stress and anxiety from your body with each breath out. It regulates your breath and heart rate as well, which allows you to calm down both mentally and physically.

With these three techniques, you should be able to give yourself some relief from your stress and anxiety by simply breathing. Being able to calm yourself with just your breath is a powerful tool because no matter where you are, you are able to help yourself.

Breathing is not like other techniques in the way that you do not need to have anything with you. You do not need to remember a specific plan or certain thoughts that may help you to calm down. You do not even need space or to be alone to use these techniques.

If you are stressed or anxious in a store, you can find help through breathing and no one will even notice. If you are having a hard time at work, you can perform these breathing exercises at your desk without your coworkers knowing. They are tools that can be used privately anywhere you go.

Chapter 14
My Morning Routine

A morning routine can be a strong tool when dealing with anxiety. It can be something that reminds your body that it is time to wake up and that it is time to have a positive day. Doing things that benefit your anxiety struggle right away in the morning can affect how your entire day goes. They can make you remember to be calm and happy. They can give you the motivation to completely defeat anxiety when it tries to enter your day.

In this chapter, I will share with you my morning routine. This routine helps me to have the best day possible. It helps me to be happy, positive, and relaxed. I will discuss what each step of this routine is, how it is done, and why it works.

Self-Care

The first part of my morning routine is self-care. I wake up, brush my teeth, have a shower, get dressed, and prepare myself for the day ahead. I do this even if I am going to stay home all day. This is an important step because when I give my body time to be cared for, I am reminded that I am important and that I am capable of accomplishing big things throughout the day.

Self-care can include anything from making yourself look nice to steps that give our body comfort, like a warm bath or nice smelling lotion. Any of these things can tell your body that it is ready to have a great day.

Meditation

After my self care routine I like to spend a few minutes meditating. This allows the body a chance to relax and reset. It takes away any worries that may have followed from the previous day and allows for a fresh start.

You can find meditations apps on your smartphone or on CD's that you can listen to. You can also use meditations that you can do on your own. Here is one of my favorites to do each morning:

"Think of, in detail, five things that you are thankful for about the day you are about to have."

This meditation allows me to not only think about my day in a positive way, but it also allows me to go within myself and feel gratitude for what I have. If I am looking forward to my day and feeling positive about the way that my life is going, I am capable of doing great things. The same goes for you. Try this meditation in the morning. I guarantee it will help how you feel about yourself and your life. It will even help you to accomplish more throughout your day if you continue to keep it in mind. Remember it is impossible to feel negative and gratitude at the same time as they are completely opposite emotions. You can only feel one so gratitude is key to controlling your mental state.

Breakfast

You can have breakfast before your meditation if you are someone that likes to eat close to when they wake up. I do intermittent fasting everyday so I have it a little later than most. When you fuel your body in the morning, it is much more capable of both feeling positive and being able to accomplish the tasks of the day that will soon begin. Having the right vitamins and nutrients in your body allow it to work in the best way possible for you, which makes it an important step in the morning routine. It's ultra important to get these nutrient into you whether you are someone that has breakfast first thing in the morning or whether you fast for a couple hours and get your breakfast in a few hours later like myself.

Conversation

The next part of my morning routine is to reach out to someone I love. This could be a family member who is eating breakfast with me or it could consist of me sending a text message to an old friend or extended family member. When I reach out to someone I love in the mornings, I know all day long that I am not alone. Any struggles that I face, I do not have to go through on my own.

This helps me to keep relationships strong as well, which is important to people who are struggling with anxiety. Because I make a point to grow relationships every day, I always have someone who I know is there to help me in the good times and the bad times alike.

Inspirational Music

Next in my morning routine, I am almost always headed to work. During my commute, I like to listen to inspirational or motivational music. This helps me to motivate myself for the upcoming day at work.

Music can be a powerful tool. It is something that we often take for granted, but I have found that the right type of music really does make a difference to my morning.

This is my morning routine and the things that I do each day benefit me in great ways. They may work for you as well so please give them a try. However, each person is different so you may need to adjust this routine to fit your needs. Some of these actions may help you, but you may need to find your own morning routine as well.

For example, some people benefit greatly from exercising right away each morning. The exercise gives them a release of endorphins and a sense of accomplishment, which they are then able to carry with them for the rest of their day. It is a healthy choice that makes their body feel good and decreases anxiety symptoms at the same time. Personally I finish my day with exercise to take any excess frustrations that I may have from my work day.

Other people like to create a to-do list in the morning. This helps them to stay on task throughout the day as well as to set goals for themselves. It gives them a sense of satisfaction and accomplishment when they are able to check these things off their list over the course of their day.

Some may also like to watch the morning news. This gives them a chance to relax and a chance to hear about what is happening in the world around them. This may allow them to feel connected and involved with their life or it might be just the break they need to start their day relaxed and refreshed.

Others like to read books. It could be an inspirational book or a book that they simply enjoy. This helps them to prepare for their day by motivating them or by giving a relaxing start to an otherwise busy day.

No matter what a part of your morning routine is, the most important thing is to simply create one. Let's look into how to do this now.

First, look at all of the examples that I have mentioned that would be good additions to a morning routine. Next, think of how much time you have in the mornings. Can you do only three things on your list or could you find time for five?

After deciding how much you can do in the mornings, decide exactly what you would like to do. Look into the possibilities and choose the activities that you know would enrich your mornings and leave a positive, lasting effect on your entire day.

Once you decide on a list, try it out! If the schedule works for you, great. If not, adjust it. Keep switching up your routine until you land on the one that feels like it fits your life perfectly.

After you find the perfect routine, make sure you stick to it. Even if you wake up tired and would rather stay in bed, remind yourself of the benefits that come from sticking to your morning routine. It will take discipline no doubt but the rewards are worth it. Keep doing it every day and watch the great effect that it has on your life.

Chapter 15
Don't Give a Shit

In life, it can be extremely hard to stop caring what others think of you. We are actually raised from an extremely young age to want those around us to be happy with us. When we were young and our parents would praise us and tell us "good job" for every little success, we started to become dependent on what others think of us. We moved away from self-intrinsic motivation and more toward getting that praise and those "good jobs".

Now as adults, it has become even harder to stop caring about what others think of us. We want to wear the right clothes, have the best house, and work the best job. We want others to see us as successful and happy even if we are not.

This motivation to make others see us as perfect people can cause a significant amount of anxiety. It causes us to portray ourselves as something we are not and to stress about how others see us.

This problem has been made way worse by the rise in popularity of social media. On sites like Facebook and Instagram, people post the good moments of their lives. They often do not post the bad things. Because of this, when you are scrolling through social media, you will most of the time see other people's success and congratulate them, while worrying about your own failure.

In all reality, you have successes as well and the other people have just as much failure. You just do not know about the low points in their life because they do not brag about them on the internet.

Let's look at an example. Your friend Sherry just posted on Facebook that she got a new house. You see this and believe that she must be doing really well financially to have this big accomplishment. You wish you could afford to buy a house like she did. Her post makes you feel bad about the financial situation that you are in.

Now, let's look behind the scenes of Sherry's post. She said that she got a house but she did not mention how hard it was to get there. She did not tell you that she now had a significant monthly debt from taking out a loan to cover her down payment. She didn't mention how she got denied by two different underwriting companies and was almost out of a place to live before the last company approved her application.

Realistically, your financial situation was not any worse than the one that Sherry was in. It may have even been better. You did not know this, however, because she only posted the good parts on Facebook.

This causes a whole new type of anxiety, but right now let's focus on not caring what others think. Did Sherry care what others thought? Yes, she did. She cared greatly about what her friends and family thought of her and posted a positive moment on Facebook to prove it.

Many of us act in similar ways. We share the good parts of our lives online to show that we are happy and successful. We do this whether it is true or not. Oftentimes even if we are miserable, we want those around us to think that we are doing good.

This behavior is not only on the internet but stems to our daily in-person lives as well. For example, at work, we may act happy even if our home lives are in a very difficult spot. We may buy clothes on a credit card that we cannot afford in order to look like we are more well off financially than we actually are. We may tell our friends about our successes in life but not about our failures.

Some people even go to as far as doing things that they do not want to do just to make others happy or make others like them. This is an unhealthy behavior that is sure to heighten the anxiety that you feel each day. If you are struggling with this, consider reaching out for help. You do not need to live life for other people.

This process gives us an unhealthy level of anxiety and in order to feel better about ourselves, we need to change it. Below we will go over some things that may help you to stop caring what other people think and start living life for no one other than yourself.

Love Yourself

The first and most important thing that you can do to make yourself stop caring about what others think is to love yourself. When you love the person that you are and the life that you choose to live, you begin to feel proud of it. You will eventually care more about what you think of your life than what others think of your life.

One thing that helps in the process of learning to love yourself is learning who you truly are. What types of things do you like? What are your favorite activities? What type of music do you listen to? Are you a cat person or a dog person?

Spend some time really getting to know yourself. When you find the things that you love and the things that make you unique, it is easier to find love for yourself.

Do Not Compare Yourself

Now that you have found ways to love and appreciate the unique individual that you truly are, try really hard to not compare yourself to others. Other people come from different circumstances. If they have the success that you envy in one area, they are likely to have the failure in an area where you excel. You each have your own specific talents and it does no good to compare them to one another. Each person is equal. No one is "better" than the true version of yourself.

Strive for Intrinsic Motivation

Next, try to make sure that the things you set out to accomplish are being done for no one but yourself. Do not do something just to impress another person if it is not something that makes you happy inside. Focus on yourself and your life. This will lessen the anxiety feeling because you will only be working to make yourself happy. You aren't making goals for them to be happy. You need to reach them for yourself.

Try to let go of the idea of pleasing others that you have been raised to do for your entire life. Try instead to please yourself. It is sure to improve how you feel about yourself and your life in general.

Take a Social Media Break

If you find yourself comparing yourself to others and constantly wanting to impress your friends on social media sites like Facebook or Instagram, consider taking a break from these sites. If you are not focused on making yourself happy, the sites are probably taking away from your quality of life. Deleting or deactivating your accounts is a simple way to make an improvement in this area of your life. You could even take a less drastic step and simply promise yourself you will not log onto your accounts until you are ready to stop caring what others think of you. This small change could make a huge difference in your life not to mention increase productivity. We don't realize how many minutes and hours you spend on social media

Overall, there are many things that you can do to start loving yourself and to stop comparing yourself to others. You can work on loving yourself, stop comparing yourself to others, search for intrinsic motivation, and take breaks from social media when necessary. Every step that you take will bring your life farther away from anxiety and closer to peace. Try the tips in our book to let go of the opinions of others. It is sure to make a significant impact in your life and in your level of happiness.

We hope that the techniques that I have shared with you in this chapter make a big change in your life. I hope that you are able to live life for yourself and not care what anyone else thinks.

Chapter 16
Food and Anxiety

As we mentioned earlier toward the very beginning of our book, there are actually certain foods and nutrients that can help ease anxiety. They can help your brain release chemicals like dopamine and serotonin, which work to make you happy. They can also help your brain to work well, think clearly, and stay calm which eases anxiety symptoms as well.

Some people turn to junk food when they are feeling stressed, but this is typically not a good choice. Cookies, cake, and other types of sugar cause energy when you first eat them, but then they cause a sugar crash later in the day. This sugar crash could actually leave you feeling more anxious than you were at the beginning of the day.

Junk food is also not a great choice because it can cause weight gain, as well as a variety of other health issues. Unhealthy foods that are filled with sugar and fats can lead to obesity, irritable bowel syndrome, diabetes, and many other diseases. They can cause your immune system to not function at its full capacity as well which can lead to you getting sick more often. Being sick, overweight, and struggling with difficult health issues are all things that can cause your anxiety to worsen significantly.

Luckily, there are foods that will do exactly the opposite of what junk foods does to us. There are foods that are healthy for our bodies and that can help to ease anxiety symptoms. These nutrients can help you to deal with stress without having a negative impact on your health or weight.

Vitamin C

One of the first things that help us with anxiety is a specific nutrient—Vitamin C. Researchers have found that when people take vitamin C before a stressful task, they had lower blood pressure and lower levels of cortisol than those who did not ingest it. This is an incredible discovery! It is amazing that something as simple as a single nutrient could be proven scientifically to help with stress.

Now, let's look into where you can find vitamin C to help with your own stress and anxiety levels. One main holder of vitamin C that many people are aware of is orange juice. People turn to this juice when they are sick for the same vitamin, but not many people know that you can turn to this juice before a stressful event to calm anxious feelings as well. Luckily, you now have this technique available to you.

All Citrus fruits are actually a fantastic source of vitamin C, including oranges, grapefruits, lemons, and limes. Other fruits and vegetables that are filled with this amazing nutrient are strawberries, kiwi, and Brussel sprouts. If these foods don't fit into your diet you can always look at using a supplement.

Zinc

Another nutrient that can help to ease your anxiety symptoms is zinc. Low levels of zinc have been linked to anxiety and depression. Meat such as beef, lamb, pork, and chicken are excellent sources of zinc, as are oysters. If you're not an oyster eater, try eating nuts and seeds. Zinc is even available as a vitamin tablet in many health food stores. There are so many ways to get this helpful nutrient that it must be worth giving it a try.

Salmon

Salmon is an extremely healthy food. It is high in protein and nutrients and low in sodium and fat. It is a meal that is easy to turn to when looking for a healthy option. It also is a meal that can help you with your anxiety symptoms.

A research study done at Ohio State University discovered that when a person takes supplements or vitamins that include Omega-3 acid, their rate at which they were experiencing stress and anxiety went down (Kiecolt-Glaser, 2011). This was also the case when the people in the study ate salmon since it is a fatty fish that is filled with these same healthy acids.

If you either do not eat or do not care for fish, try taking an Omega-3 acid supplement. It may make you see a huge difference in your struggle with stress and anxiety.

Pink Himalayan Salt

Pink Himalayan Salt is said to have ions that can create a positive atmosphere, which in return benefits your mood and decreases symptoms or anxiety (Taddia, 2014).

You may recognize this type of salt from the currently trending salt lamps. The lamps are said to have this ion that creates a positive atmosphere when other things around us can cause a negative one.

Consuming Pink Himalayan Salt can do the same job. This salt can simply be used instead of typical white table salt. It tastes the same and works in the same way for your cooking, so it is a very simple substitute.

The nice thing about using this substitute is that it helps you to feel positive and at the same time reduces the struggle that you face with anxiety.

Pink Himalayan Salt can be used in many ways from eating it to salt lamps to adding it to your nightly bath. No matter how you use it, it should have a positive effect on your quality of life.

Avocado

Avocado is a food that people have recently started to love more than ever. This might have more to do with its healthy place in a balanced diet, and its ability to make great guacamole than anything else, but avocado is actually also really great for easing the symptoms of anxiety.

Avocado helps with anxiety because it contains B vitamins (Shelton, 2018). These B vitamins are actually linked to happier and healthier lifestyles. Avocados also contain a healthy source of fat that is both beneficial to your heart and into your brain. When you give your brain the nutrients that it needs, it is able to function at a higher level. When your brain is able to function at a higher level, you may experience fewer symptoms of anxiety, simply because your brain has what it needs to take care of you in the best way that it possibly can.

So next time you are out with your friends and you want to indulge in some delicious guacamole, feel free to do so. Remember that you are not just indulging but actually helping your brain and easing your anxiety symptoms at the same time. What a wonderful food that can benefit our body in so many ways!

We can now see that there are many nutrients and foods that can support our body and our fight against anxiety. But did you know that there is actually a lifestyle change and a way of eating that can benefit your mental health as well? The keto diet has been said to ease anxiety symptoms alongside all of these nutrients that we mentioned above.

The Keto Diet

This way of eating is called the keto diet or the ketogenic diet. It is consist of eating basically no carbs or a very low amount of carbs. Instead, the people on this diet eat mostly foods that contain high levels of fat. This seems like a diet that would make someone gain weight, but it actually does the opposite.

The ketogenic diet causes people on it to lose weight by means of ketosis. Ketosis is a stage that your body goes through if you have eaten a lot of fat and it causes you to burn off that fat and more (Eenfeldt, 2019).

This type of diet cannot only make you lose weight, but it can also help your struggle with anxiety. The keto diet helps with anxiety because it has a high-fat intake. As we mentioned earlier, fatty foods allow your brain to function at its highest possible level. When your brain is functioning as well as it can, it is able to help you get through your anxiety easier than you could otherwise. It allows you to think clearly and to not worry about things that do not matter. Anyone who struggles with anxiety knows that being able to not worry will help their symptoms significantly.

Because the keto diet is so capable of helping people with anxiety to lessen the symptoms, let's look at a few tips for successfully following this way of eating and look into some delicious recipes that you may want to try out as well.

Recipes

Addicting Chicken - Keto Style

We all love things filled with cream cheese and bacon, but are they not sure to be bad for us? That's what it seems like, but if you are doing the ketogenic diet, this recipe may help you to succeed.

It is filled with fats that will help your anxiety level as well. This is definitely a win-win situation. It's a healthy meal and a healthy brain! You will not be able to find many things better than that.

The first ingredient in this recipe is of course, chicken. It is actually kind of cool because you can make the chicken in many different ways. You can use already cooked or leftover chicken if you have it. If you do it this way, the meal will be made extremely fast since you would not have to wait for the chicken to finish cooking.

You can also use raw or frozen chicken. The chicken can be cooked in the oven or on top of the stove, in a crock pot, or in an instant pot. This recipe can really be made in any way that you feel the most comfortable.

After you cook the chicken, you will want to shred it. You could use anything from forks to a blender—it really is simply up to you.

You then add the rest of the ingredients to give your shredded chicken an amazing flavor. You will add cream cheese, bacon, ranch powder or your own homemade ranch seasoning mix, and cheddar cheese. You can warm the ingredients in any means that you are comfortable with and have time to use. If you're short on time, consider using a pressure cooker or instant pot. If you are cooking early in the day to prep for dinner, consider using a crock pot. If you have a typical amount of time or do not have either of these two devices, using your oven or stovetop will work just fine.

This recipe is great alone or served on top of other Keto-friendly foods like cabbage, broccoli, zucchini noodles, spinach or cauliflower to add even more nutrients.

Ingredients:

- Two pieces of bacon cut into small chunks
- Two pounds of chicken with no skin and no bones
- 16 ounces of cream cheese
- .5 cups of plain water
- 2 tbsp of vinegar, preferably apple cider
- 1 tbsp chives
- 1.5 tbsp powdered garlic
- 1.25 tbsp powdered onion
- 1 tsp flakes of red pepper
- 1 tsp dill
- .25 tsp salt
- .25 tsp pepper
- .5 cup of cheddar, shredded
- 1 sliced scallion

How to Make

1. Cook chicken
2. Shred chicken
3. Add other ingredients
4. Cook to bring together

I hope you love this Keto style Addicting Chicken recipe! It is delicious and will help ease your anxiety as well.

The next recipe we will look at is:

Deviled Eggs with Bacon and Blue Cheese

Deviled eggs are typically a treat that we get on holidays, not something we can eat as a snack year round. They are typically not healthy for us, but this recipe changes that completely because it follows the Ketogenic diet.

This deviled egg recipe is a twist on the original since it adds in the flavors of bacon and blue cheese. It's a delicious combination that you will surely enjoy.

Luckily, it comes with the added bonus of helping you with your anxiety because it is Keto and contains many healthy fats. It also helps with anxiety even more than other Keto foods because eggs are said to relieve stress as well, thanks to how nutrient-filled they are. Let's look into how to make this delicious and helpful treat:

Ingredients

- 8 eggs, hard-boiled in water
- .25 c of sour cream
- .33 c of mayo
- 1 tbsp of mustard, preferably Dijon flavor
- .5 tsp salt
- .25 tsp pepper
- .25 tsp dill
- .25 c blue cheese, works best if it's crumbled
- 3 pieces of bacon, already cooked and cut into chunks
- Optional parsley for on top the eggs

How to make this meal

1. Cut every one of your eight eggs in half
2. Scoop out the yoke
3. Put the yokes together in a bowl

4. Mash up the yokes with a fork or similar utensil
5. Add in the rest of the ingredients and stir
6. Add more mayo if the ingredients seem dry
7. Fill the egg whites with the mix you just made
8. Sprinkle with parsley if you would like to
9. Enjoy!

This was again a great recipe to help our bodies and our minds. Let's look into one more recipe together in this book.

Everyone loves pizza. Just because you were on the keto diet doesn't mean you should live without this delicious meal. This recipe gives us a low-carb version of pizza that you can enjoy while still participating in the ketogenic diet.

Keto Pizza

This pizza is low-carb because the crust is made out of simply eggs and cheese. It does not include carbs at all, but it still gives you the pizza that you may be craving since you can't have a normal crust on this diet. The crust is made differently but the rest of the pizza can be made just like any other pizza would be.

Ingredients

- 4 eggs
- Shredded cheese - 1 cup
- Three tablespoons of tomato paste
- One teaspoon of dried oregano
- Cheese to top
- Toppings you enjoy such as meat or vegetables

How to make Keto Pizza

In order to make this pizza, you need to start by preheating your oven to 400°. While the oven is preheating, you will want to start making the crust. The process of making the crust only includes putting in the eggs and cheese in a bowl and stirring them together.

Once you make your cheese and egg mixture, you want to dump it onto a baking sheet. You may want to use tin-foil or paper on the bottom of the pan so that the pizza crust doesn't stick to it. You can make your pizza into any shape you want it to be. You can make it the size of the pan or you can make mini circle pizzas for fun.

After you get the crust ready, bake it for 15 minutes. You will then raise the temperature of the oven to 450°. While this is heating, you will want to spread your sauce onto your crust. You will then sprinkle oregano spices onto the sauce. Once your sauce creation is complete, you can top the pizza with the cheese that you like and the toppings that you prefer. Some ideas for pizza varieties would be pepperoni and sausage, plain cheese, or a veggie pizza.

Once you have made your pizza the way that you want it, you can put it back into the oven at 450° for between five and 10 minutes. The time that your pizza is in the oven may depend on your specific type of oven and how well it works. You will want to watch your pizza and take it out when it is starting to turn golden and look the way that you want it to be when you eat it.

You can eat this pizza alone or you can eat it with a side salad to add even more nutrients into your meal.

Pizza usually it's not a healthy dinner, so this keto pizza is a pretty exciting thing to find. It helps your body to be healthy, as well as your mind.

If you are looking for foods that will help you to ease your anxiety symptoms, I encourage you to try out the recipes that I have given you in this book. I believe that they will help you feel better and less stressed. The keto diet has been proven to help with stress and anxiety, which is why I believe it will help in your life as well.

Alongside these meals, you can try to incorporate the nutrients and foods that we found to be beneficial for your anxiety levels into your meal plans as well. Anxiety can be a hard thing to deal with, but when you tackle it from every side, including nutrition and what you eat, you will be able to overcome it.

If you are looking for a good "how to start" guide to the Keto diet, the book "Simple Easy Keto" by Michele Moranti is a good one from the amazon store or audible.com.

Chapter 17
Exercise and Anxiety

Exercise can be a difficult thing for people to partake in, but it truly does benefit our health in so many ways. One of these ways is by improving our mental health and lessening anxiety symptoms. We will focus in this chapter on how moving your body can improve your quality of life.

It is actually incredible that something as simple as exercise can benefit your life in so many ways. It has been proven to help with stress and anxiety. It can help you if you suffer from anxiety-related symptoms like fatigue as well.

Even though stress is in your brain, we know that it affects your body as well. This is because your brain has nerves that go to the rest of your body. When the nerves are affected by stress, physical symptoms begin to show.

Exercise has been proven to not only lower the tension levels in your body but decrease the anxiousness in your mind as well. It can help you to feel happier as well as better about yourself. It can improve confidence and self-esteem, which in turn helps with lessening anxiety even more.

If you have spent any time exercising in your life, you know that this science makes sense. When you finish exercising, you get a rush of endorphins and you begin to feel happier and more relaxed. You will also get a sense of accomplishment which can make you feel like your day was worthwhile, making you feel less stress. This sense of accomplishment can even lessen your anxiety because it shows you that you are capable of succeeding in big things. This could make the things you are anxious about seem much less scary.

Relationship of Exercise to Anxiety Disorders

We know that stress is common. Stressful situations arise in the life of every single person on Earth. Stress is simply a part of life and it's not something that a person can avoid forever. Did you know, though, that anxiety is extremely common as well? It is actually the most common mental illness that people suffer from today. Luckily, exercise can help almost anyone who struggles with this disorder.

Scientists have actually proven that exercise reduces the amount of anxiety symptoms that we feel. It helps our bodies to tolerate stress better because when we treat our bodies well, they are able to perform at their best for us. Exercise also releases chemicals like serotonin into your brain to allow you to feel happy. When you're happy, you are more optimistic and you are able to handle stress and anxiety much easier than if you were feeling down.

Again, these studies will make sense once you have given exercise a try. It truly can make a big difference in how you feel about yourself and about your life. As far as my own journey goes I found exercise along with diet to be the number 1 combination to help me beat stress and anxiety. Throw journaling on top of this and it completely changed my mindset and life.

Exercise as Part of Therapy

There are many ways to treat anxiety and its symptoms. As long as you are making safe and healthy choices, there are no wrong ways to treat your symptoms. For example, some people tend to benefit the most from therapy or talking to someone they love about what they are going through in their life. Other people tend to do best when they take a medication that is made to help specifically with anxiety. Others yet may do best with exercise.

Exercise can be a great part of your therapy routine if you are currently struggling with stress or with an anxiety disorder and the great thing is it's instant. Try adding workouts into your day if you can. Here are some workouts that you could try:

Walking

Walking is a great form of exercise for many people. It is a great starting point if you have not been staying in shape recently. It is easy to do, it's free, doesn't involve a gym membership or equipment and you can do it anywhere, so there really are no excuses as to why this workout cannot be at least tried. Try walking for twenty minutes. If you feel up to it, change your speed while you walk. Move your legs fast for one minute, then slow the next. This will help you to get even more from your time spent moving.

Jogging

If you are looking for a challenge above walking, try running or jogging. You could even sign up for a community race or fun run to motivate yourself. Pick a speed or distance that you would like to accomplish and work toward it. You will feel extremely proud of yourself when you reach your goal. Having a goal or a focus for the future is great for keeping your mind off other issues you are facing. I normally do fun runs and use it to raise money for different charities I like. This gives me a focus, keeps me fit and the fact I'm doing something for people less fortunate than myself also makes me feel good about myself. It's a win/win.

To mix up your running routine, try different workouts. Try running some sprints on a football field one day and taking a long, slow jog the next day. Try pushing yourself to run some hill repeats on the largest slope in your neighborhood. If you get bored, try a new path or run with a friend.

Sports

If you need some added fun to motivate yourself to exercise, consider joining a sports team. There are many options for sports like softball, volleyball, and bowling that you could get involved with. This not only adds a new level of fun to your workout but adds accountability and friendship as well from being a part of a team. Look around in your community for teams that you could be a part of.

Gyms

If you live in a cold weather area, need to exercise early in the morning or late at night, or simply enjoy working out indoors, consider joining a gym. You can use their equipment to focus on cardio or strength training. Many gyms even have personal trainers or group fitness classes that you could be a part of for added motivation and accountability.

Online Workout Videos

If you are not yet comfortable working out in front of other people or are for any reason unable to leave your home for exercise, try following along with some online workout videos. There are workouts available for free on sites like YouTube and paid subscriptions available on sites like Netflix or Beachbody. These workouts are nice because they can be done at home with little or no equipment and they can be done in a short amount of time. This makes it seem like there is no excuse to not moving your body at least a little bit.

Even if you do not have a specific plan for exercise, just go outside and take a walk down your street or around your yard. Something as simple as this can benefit your mental health just as much as a complex workout. When you get outside and begin to breathe fresh air, you will likely begin to feel happier naturally. When you start to move your body, you will feel even happier. Even just this simple exercise is good for both your mental and physical health.

When you are moving your body and you become physically healthier, anxiety is sometimes easier to manage. If you feel good, you may feel more capable of taking on the things that scare you. If you are not struggling with the many health issues that come from a lack of physical activity, you will have fewer worries on your mind.

If you do not feel motivated to walk, you could simply play catch with your son or daughter or go outside with your pets. Any type of movement is better than none. And who knows, once you start, you may not want to stop!

Chapter 18
Moving Forward

We have covered a significant amount of information in this book that will help you to live a better life even though you struggle with anxiety. The information that I have gone over can help you to decrease your level of anxiety or even overcome it completely. Now it's time to go through a review so that we can remember what we have covered together.

We started out this book looking at the different types of anxiety. Anxiety comes in many forms from social anxiety, generalized anxiety, and panic attacks. The way that you handle your specific version of anxiety depends on the type that you struggle with and the severity.

We then looked into shyness versus social anxiety. We learned that shyness and social anxiety are very different things. Shyness is a normal reaction to have as a human and it is often a part of a person's personality. Shyness is not a negative feature to have. If you are shy and you do not like being shy, there are many activities that you can do to help yourself overcome your shyness. It is important to remember, however, that shyness is not a mental illness and is not something that needs to be overcome unless the person wants to change it.

Social anxiety, on the other hand, is a mental illness and is often something that people want to fix when they struggle with it. Social anxiety is a much more severe topic than shyness. It can make the lives of the people who struggle with it very difficult and it can hold them back from taking part in activities that they otherwise would love to do.

If you struggle with social anxiety, look back to this chapter and implement the tips that i have given into your life. If you feel it is necessary, feel free to reach out to a medical professional or even myself in the Facebook group to help you with your struggles. Social anxiety is not something that you need to suffer through alone.

Next, we looked into symptoms of anxiety. We learned that anxiety can have symptoms that are physical, cognitive, and behavioral. We talked about how people with anxiety can experience any number of symptoms. People without anxiety can have these symptoms as well but not to the severity that people with anxiety have. If you have the symptoms and do not struggle with them on a daily basis, you probably do not struggle from an anxiety disorder. If you do struggle with these symptoms often and they impact the way that you live your daily life, you may want to look into getting help to treat your anxiety disorder. A mental health professional would be able to help you and the tips in this book should be able to get you started on a journey towards a healthy life.

Next, we looked into the fact that anxiety might not actually be a problem. The problem that you were facing might be low self-esteem and you may be having anxiety as a defense mechanism against the judgments that you are feeling toward yourself. As I mentioned in this chapter this was very much so the case myself.

We then talked about how a lot of anxiety can stem from past events. You may be affected from something that you went through as a child or a young adult. It helps to talk through these things so that you know longer struggle with them. It is important to note, however, that post-traumatic stress disorder is different than anxiety. If you struggle with PTSD, please reach out to get help from a medical professional.

We then looked at the fear of rejection, another vice of mine, and how it can have an effect on anxiety in your life. Almost everyone is afraid of rejection but sometimes this fear can be so crippling that it affects our ability to try to get the things that we want in life. This can result in us not going for the jobs that we want and it can also end up in us not fulfilling the relationships that we want to have. If the fear of rejection is hurting your life and the choices that you want to make, look into this chapter and try to find some tips that will help you in your struggle.

Then we looked into anticipation and how it is always worse than the outcome. We often feel anxiety symptoms the most when we are at home waiting for an event to happen. We look at the event in our minds and we picture all of the horrible things that could happen even if logically none of them would ever actually happen to us.

This chapter provides tips to deal with anticipation and how to not worry so much about future events. If you are struggling with anticipation and worrying about your future, please look into this chapter for techniques that can help you.

We talked about how stress and anxiety are different but they can often feel the same. Stress can often lead to anxiety as well. Both struggles can cause physical, cognitive, and behavioral struggles. They can both have symptoms that interrupt our lives significantly and keep us from living the way we want to live. In this chapter, we go into detail on how to manage stress and give you tips and tools that you will be able to use in your daily life.

Next, we looked into journaling. I think this was one of the most important chapters in the book as I really rate journaling as an effective method of overcoming anxiety and pretty much any mental health issue. We looked into the research behind why journaling helps so much with anxiety and how science proves that it is an amazing tool. We talked about how to start journaling, as well as look into examples of what a journal entry might look like. We discussed that our journal entries will change over time and become more and more detailed and contain more emotion as we get better at the process. Once we become good at journaling, we will learn a lot about ourselves and about how we are feeling by writing our thoughts down. To move forward you need to know where you have been and understand where your at currently and why. Journaling is great for achieving that.

We talked about repetition and how practicing the ways in which we can overcome our fears can be extremely beneficial. We discussed that it is possible for you to replay situations over in your mind or actually try the situations until you are no longer afraid of them. We talked about examples and tips and tricks on how to do this.

We then talked about location-specific social anxiety. We talked about how anxiety can come in locations like parties, offices or workplaces, places where we need to participate in public speaking, shopping malls, and sales related activities.

We talked about how we can relieve each of these different types of social anxieties. We have discussed tools for each of the locations including parties and workplaces and talked about how we can feel comfortable in these environments even though that may sound like a difficult task today.

We discussed how to do small talk because this can be a very frustrating and scary thing for many people. I gave you many tips and tricks on how to successfully participate in small talk and went through lots of examples so that you can feel comfortable next time you try. Small talk is often a very scary topic for people so this chapter may be helpful to many of you and I encourage you to go back to it and use the tools that I have provided.

We looked into breathing exercises and how they can help to control your emotional state of being. We looked at breathing exercises from ancient times and breathing exercises that are often referred to in medical practices today. I taught you how to do these exercises and I encourage you to implement them into your daily routine.

Speaking of routines, we then looked at having a morning routine. We looked at my specific morning routine and what I do to feel confident in my day. We then looked into different morning routine items that may help you and discussed the best way for you to build a routine that really starts your day off on the right foot.

After that, we discussed not caring what other people think of us. We looked into how our society is changing and how we always post positive things on social media but we never post the negative things on social media. We talked about how this hurts our self-esteem and makes us seem like we are less successful than those around us when really we are just not seeing the negative parts of their lives. We spoke about how if you are struggling with this, it may be a good idea to take a break from social media sites like Facebook and Instagram. I also gave tips on how to love yourself and how to stop comparing yourself to others which should help you to not care what they think. You are an amazing person and you will feel much less anxious once you realize that about yourself.

We also talked about different foods and how they can help anxiety. We looked into nutrients and foods like vitamin C and avocados. We then looked into the ketogenic diet and how it can help with anxiety. We looked at recipes that are delicious and healthy for your brain.

Lastly, we looked into exercise and how moving your body can help decrease stress and anxious feelings. We looked at workouts that you can do to make yourself feel less stressed and the science behind why exercise helps our brains so much.

Conclusion

To conclude this book today, I want to thank you for reading and spending this much time with me. I hope that the tips in our book were extremely helpful and that you are able to lessen your anxiety symptoms or completely overcome your anxiety disorder altogether because of them. I hope that if these tips and tricks are not enough, that you seek help from a medical professional because life does not need to be as hard as it is right now for you. I want you to have a happy and stress-free life. We know that it is hard in today's society, but it is my goal to help you to reach that pointer as close to it as possible.

I hope that my research behind anxiety disorders and their symptoms has helped you to discover the things that you are struggling with and I hope that you were able to get to know yourself better over the course of this book. If you know yourself better, you will be able to help yourself better.

As I have mentioned many times throughout this book, you are not alone. You have friends and family, who if you reach out to them, would be more than happy to care for you and help you along in this journey. You also have professional help if you would like to use it. Never feel like you were alone in this battle because you never will be. Unfortunately this is a problem that is becoming more and more common as time goes by.

Remember even though you struggle with anxiety, you are an amazing person inside and out. Like all of us you have a lot to add to this world and your struggles with mental illness do not define you as a person and you are capable of amazing things. You can overcome this and you can accomplish all of your goals. I hope that this book helps you with that realization.

If you enjoyed this book and benefit from our tips and tricks, please review us on Amazon. This will help us to reach more people and help everyone who is in need.

References

https://www.ncbi.nlm.nih.gov/pmc/articles/PMC3208958/

https://www.dietdoctor.com/recipes/keto-pizza

https://www.lvhn.org/

http://theconversation.com/to-reduce-stress-and-anxiety-write-your-happy-thoughts-down-99349

https://mymorningroutine.com/

https://www.dietdoctor.com/low-carb/keto

https://www.psycom.net/foods-that-help-with-anxiety-and-stress/

http://trueformlife.com/detox-stress-himalayan-salt/

https://www.mensjournal.com/food-drink/can-eating-salmon-cure-anxiety-0/

https://www.verywellmind.com/the-benefits-of-journaling-for-stress-management-3144611

www.ingramcontent.com/pod-product-compliance
Lightning Source LLC
Chambersburg PA
CBHW032045290426
44110CB00012B/964